GW00731364

Young

POETRY MATTERS

Edited by Jenni Bannister

Poems From England

First published in Great Britain in 2011 by:

 Young**Writers**

Remus House
Coltsfoot Drive
Peterborough
PE2 9BF
Telephone: 01733 890066
Website: www.youngwriters.co.uk

All Rights Reserved
Book Design by Samantha Wood
© Copyright Contributors 2011
SB ISBN 978-0-85739-347-0

Foreword

Since our inception in 1991, Young Writers has endeavoured to promote poetry and creative writing within schools by running annual nationwide competitions. These competitions are designed to develop and nurture the burgeoning creativity of the next generation, and give them valuable confidence in their own abilities.

This regional anthology is one of the series produced by our latest secondary school competition, *Poetry Matters*. Using poetry as their tool, the young writers were given the opportunity to tell the world what matters to them. The authors of our favourite three poems were also given the chance to appear on the front cover of their region's collection.

Whilst skilfully conveying their opinions through poetry, the writers showcased in this collection have simultaneously managed to give poetry a breath of fresh air, brought it to life and made it relevant to them. Using a variety of themes and styles, our featured poets leave a lasting impression of their inner thoughts and feelings, making this anthology a rare insight into the next generation.

Contents

Bishop Ullathorne Catholic School, Coventry
Sophie Harding (12) 1
Hannah Power (12) 2

Bryanston School, Blandford Forum
Niamh Simpson (13) 3

Burlington Danes Academy, London
Victor Vilela (13) 4
Abigail Asante 5

Buxton School, Leytonstone
Dami Aberuagba (12) 5
Parys Lanlehin Dobson (15) 6
Dominique Joseph (13) 8

Calday Grange Grammar School, West Kirby
Matt Page (13) 9
Charlie Quinn (14) 10
Chris Marland (13) 11
Will O'Leary (13) 12
Daniel Ibrahim (13) 12
Luke Needham (13) 13
Joe McNeill (13) 14
Adam Clift (12) 16
Jamie Duggan (12) 16
James Martin (12) 17
Alexander Craig (12) 17
Jacob Wright (12) 18
Matthew Clare (12) 19
Jack Sanders (12) 20
Jonathan Tam (14) 20
Robert Herbertson (12) 21
Danny Mabon (12) 22
Joseph Schiller (13) 22
Deane O'Shaughnessy (13) 23
Joshua Sutton & Adam Clift (12) 24

George Kenny (12) 25
Harry Broadhurst (12) 25
Will Broadbelt (13) 26
Tom Cameron (11) 26
Paul Maddocks (12) 27
George Tipton (11) 28
Nathan Kellner (13) 29
Daniel Atherton (13) 30
Maxwell Shaw (13) 30
Kurush Medhora (13) 31
Harry Hall (13) 32
Ben Acton (12) 32
Alexander Youngson (11) 33
Jack Turner (13) 33
Felipe Pacheco (13) 34
Michael Simpson (13) 36
Matthew Hale (13) 37
Harry Das (11) 38
Alexander Congdon (11) 38
Aidan Dunn (13) 39
Luke Williams (14) 40
Michael Pritchard-Howarth (13) 41
Dom Mazhindu (13) 42
Rafael Cavallini (13) 43
Audley Cruttenden (14) 44
Jacob Swan (13) 45
David Eckl (13) 46
Jake Mathot (11) 47
Shasank Loharuka (11) 48
Ben Hamlett (11) 49
Robert Love (12) 50
Conor Clements (12) 51
Will Gibson (11) 52
Miles Knoop (11) 53

Oliver Kelly [13]......................................54
Lee Churchill [12] 55
Jack Leary [12] 56

Edmonton County School, London
Daniel Francis [13] 56
Janan Kolcak [13].....................................57
Kayleigh Small [13] 57
Jasmine Eames [13]...................................58

Eggbuckland Community College, Plymouth
Joe Benjamin Dwerryhouse [11] 60
Tolon Andrews [11]....................................61
Christopher Smith [11]..............................62

Glenmoor School for Girls, Bournemouth
Margarita Tolstaya [13]..............................63
Tia Wells [13] 64

Hillcrest School, Birmingham
Hillery Phillip [12]....................................65
Jade Loxton [12] 66
Patricia Tamayem [12] 66

Hitchin Girls' School, Hitchin
Jasmine Pandit [11] 67
Hannah Malyon [13] 67
Shamma Dalal [13] 68
Yasmin Gariba-Hamilton [11] 70
Sophie Harris [11] 70
Abbie Clarke [11] 71
Millie Morris [16] 71
Amy Saunders [16] 72
Imogen Richardson [14] 73
Josie Thomas [14] 74
Samantha Rawlings [11] 75

Hodge Hill School, Birmingham
Ghazi Ali [15]...75

Holbrook High School, Ipswich
Cecily Cullen [11] 76
Tom Harmer [11] 76
Emerson Lee-Scott [11]..............................77
Alfie Vaughan [11] 78
Aoife Treacy [11] 79
Sarah Roberts [11] 79
Kyle Hammersley [11] 80
Dani Mills [11]..81

Ibstock Place School, London
Helen Sychta [12].....................................82

King Arthur's Community School, Wincanton
Rhiannon Griffiths [13]..............................82
Asie Jakubowa [13] 83
Hollie Biss [12] 83
Catherine Parker [14] 84
Holly Turk [13]...85
Samantha Hurlow [13] 86
Lauren Armson [12] 87
Frank Higgins [11] 87
George Heal [12].......................................88
Matthew Callard-Weller [12] 89
Abi Butt [12] 90
Clare Ashford [11].....................................92

King Edward VI Handsworth School, Birmingham
Georgina Ramsay [12]................................92

Middlewich High School, Middlewich
Amy Grierson [12] 93
Katie Connell [11].....................................93
Mya Cross [12] 94
Megan Berey [11] 94
Katie Lightfoot [11]...................................95
Morgan Harrison [11]................................95
Natasha Harrop [11]..................................96
Kyran Gibson [12] 96
Chloe Scott [12]..97

Newton Abbot College, Newton Abbot
Liam Hill (16) 98
Rachel Spooner (12) 99
Catline Hill (14)....................................100

Oaklands Catholic School, Waterlooville
David Sparrow (13)................................102

Paddington Academy, London
Hilla Hamidi (11)..................................102
Nural Ismail (11) 103
Mayharun Nessa (11)..............................103
Tania Mufti (11) 104
Arza Zenuni (11)..................................104
Jade Thomas (13) 105

Peter Symonds College, Winchester
Timothy Manton (17)..............................106

Richard Lander School, Truro
Lewis Pilcher (15)................................107
Danyal Ley-Seccombe (11).........................107
Jonathan Wills (11)...............................108
Kieran Smith (11) 108
Alabama Seymour (11).............................109
Mathew Tapson (11)...............................109
Nathan Hope (14) 110
Matthew Troughton (11)...........................110
Zak Hubbard (11).................................111
Hannah Whitworth (11) 111
Jade Varley (12) 112
Luke Waters (11)..................................112
Charlie Merrifield (11) 113
Ben Kent (13).....................................113
Chloe Ellul (13) 114
Mason Ireland (13) 115
Oscar Mackenzie (13) 115
Ben Keane (13) 116
Paris Scott (12)...................................116
Alex Fryett (13)...................................117
Harry Lawrence (12)...............................117

Shannon Gray (14) 118
Sarah Bennett (13) 118
Jed Hope (13) 119
Daniel Roberson (11) 119
Alexandrea Hunter (13)............................120
Jodie MacQueen (13)..............................120
Jennifer Lovering (13) 121
Katie Platts (12) 121
Harry Searle (13) 122
Adam Britland (13)................................123
Louis Mavor (15)..................................124
Natasha Brookes (15)..............................125
Bethany Howell (15)...............................126
Jago Penrose (14) 126
Fraser Hill (13) 127
Reece Light (13)..................................128
Elijah Francis (13) 128
Erin Lynn (13) 129
Kerenza Cattell (12)..............................129
Jacob Englefield (13)..............................130
Aaron Crowhurst (12) 131
Jimi Harrold (12).................................132
Leanna Rees (12).................................133
Jonathan Brown (12)..............................133
Mollie Jewell (12)................................134
Luther Wolf (13)..................................134
Ellie Faux (12)...................................145
Rose Pipkin......................................145
Tamzin Knuckey (13)..............................146
Megan Lee (15) 147
Rebecca Pearce (14)..............................148
Benjamin Smith (12)..............................148
Eden Pilcher (13).................................149
Lauren Wroe (12).................................149
Amy Stephens (14)................................150
Molly Kirton (14).................................150
Amber Tithecott (14)..............................151
Josh Maloy (14)..................................152
Chelsea Humby (13) 152

Chloe Sobey [14].....................................153
Jonathan Russell [12]..............................153
Paige Brown [12]....................................154
Courtney Smith [12]................................154
Dylan Pina-Hoblyn [12]...........................155
Louis Downing [12].................................155

St Bede's RC Middle School, Redditch
Amelia Ebanks [12]..................................156
Kieran Kite [12].......................................157
Jaynaya Cox [12].....................................158
Ellie Brown [13]......................................159
Niall Lindsey & Kelan Hawkeswood 160
William Harris [12]...................................161
Liam Smith [12].......................................162
Mollie Louise Ralph [12]...........................163
Whitney Harris [12].................................164
Rebecca Jones [12]..................................165
Seamus Townsend [12].............................166
Georgia Smyth]12]..................................167
Nicole Sutton [12]...................................168
Annabelle Johnstone [12].........................169
Emily Blakemore [12]...............................170
Owen Wiseman [12].................................171
Owen Boggis [12].....................................172

St Michael's Catholic Grammar School, London
Hannah El-Hawary [13]............................173
Sorcha Leavey [11]..................................174
Rebecca Tyrrell [11].................................176
Miriam Yemane [11].................................177
Kathryn O'Connell [11].............................178
Beth Asante [11].....................................179

St Osmund's CE (Aided) Middle School, Dorchester
Holly Donnell [12]....................................179
Lauren Steele [12]...................................180
Grace Osborne [11]..................................181
Lucy Bone [11]...182

Lucy Harron [12].....................................184
Nikki Hills [12]..185
Hannah Smalldon [12]..............................185
Shona Sealy [12].....................................186
Emma Murgatroyd [12].............................187
Lucy Walker [12].....................................188
Jack Davies [12]......................................189
Eilish Hart [12].......................................190
Jack Cartwright [12].................................191
Catherine Simmons [12]...........................192
Anabel Mitchem [13]................................193
Chloe Neil [12]..194
Robert Adams [12]...................................194
Joss Minterne [12]...................................195
Sam Dance [11].......................................195
Ellie Smith [12].......................................196
Leah Dear [12]..196
Rachel Smith [13]....................................197
Ellen Porter [12].....................................198
Liam Churchill [12]..................................198
Esther Kagi [11]......................................199
Poppy Hosford [11]..................................200
John Reedie [12]......................................201
Hannah Wyatt [12]...................................201
Dan Davies [12].......................................202
Melissa Merritt [12].................................202
Dan Thomson [12]....................................203
Laura Barrett [11]....................................203
Georgia Mae Daw [12]..............................204
Rebecca Hawkins [11]..............................204
Flora Johnson [11]...................................205
Aislin Fields [11].....................................205
Ross Guy [12]..206
Christopher Ninham [12]...........................208
Ellie Chambers [11].................................209
Aldo D'Arrigo [11]...................................210
Eloise Carter [11]....................................210
Ben Macklin [11].....................................211

St Wilfrid's School, Exeter
Jordan Mitchell [11] 212
Aja Humphries [12] 213
Matthew Heathcote [12] 214
Emily Piper [11] 216
Laura Wells [12] 217
James Dutton [13] 218
Elliot Dawson [12] 219

Sarah Bonnell School, Stratford
Deborah Adebola [12] 220
Nisha Kaur [11] 221
Shanjidah Ahad [12] 222
Mythily Nagarajah [12] 223
Hanna Girma [11] 223
Tyler Cormack [12] 224
Nazia Rahman [12] 225
Sanjidah Chowdhury [11] 225
Nicole Cook [11] 226
Aamna Ali [12] 226
Afsana Begum [11] 227
Jumana Ahmed [11] 228

Sir John Cass Foundation & Red Coat School, London
Sakeen Zaman [15] 229
Tamanna Khanum [16] 229
Dilwar Hussain [17] 230
Nazifa Begum [15] 231
Fahim Rahman [15] 232

The American School In London, London
Meredith Bertasi [16] 233

The Clere School, Newbury
Katherine Tweed [13] 234
Eli Hatter [12] 235
Nicholas Tate [12] 236
Victoria Chappell [12] 236
Chloe Long [12] 237
Luke Skeels [12] 237

Matthew Pawley [12] 238
Louise Collins [12] 239
Jemma Mead [12] 239
Elizabeth Wilcox [12] 240
Barnaby Smeddle [12] 240
Natasha Everest [12] 241
Jessica Emberlin [13] 242
Edwin Edwards [12] 243
Ffion Donoghue [12] 243
Katherine Best [12] 244
Toby Carter [12] 245
Alexandra Humphreys [12] 246
Chloe Bryan [12] 247
Maddie Christy [11] 247
Mollie Lawrence [12] 248
Grace Goslin [12] 249
Megan Broughton [13] 250
Anna Maria Markiewicz [12] 251
Theo Canes [11] 252
Catherine Wellington [11] 252
Thomas Hall [13] 253
Sarah Ladd [12] 254
Rosie King [13] 256
Elke Abinger [12] 257
Alexandra Winter [13] 257
Zoe Baronius Bevan [13] 258
Katie Scott [15] 259
Justine Whitehead [11] 259
Luke Williams [11] 260
Katie Sainsbury [14] 260
Tom Price [14] 261
Faye Lillywhite-Buley [11] 261
Christopher Spence [13] 262
Megan Dalgarno [13] 263
James Medcraft [11] 264
John Anderson [13] 265
Jack Allen [11] 266
Aisha Baizid [11] 266
Louis Hooper [11] 267

The Isle of Wight College, Newport

Claudia Fuller (17).. 268

Lydia Freya Lowrence Lee (16).................................. 269

Michael Sims (17) 270

Rachael Wade (18) 271

Karen Elliott (16) 272

Sarah Redrup (16) 274

The Wey Valley School, Weymouth

Charlotte West (11) 275

Paige Sewell (13).. 276

Kay Conway-Smith (13) 276

Torquay Boys' Grammar School, Torquay

Eliot Glanvill (16)..277

Joe Bennett (16) 278

The Poems

My Bear

I've had this bear for a while,
Actually since I was born.
He started off shiny and new,
Now he's old and torn.

His soft body is pink,
The fur on his head is white,
He has a ribbon wrapped round his neck
And it's done up in a bow really tight.

I went to hospital with him,
About when I was two.
I had broken my wrist on a bouncy castle,
Which is unusual for a child to do.

He is a special part of my childhood,
He'll stay with me for all of my days.
So even when I'm older,
In a corner of my heart he stays.

Sophie Harding (12)
Bishop Ullathorne Catholic School, Coventry

My Birthday

On my birthday I wake
with a smile,
I run downstairs to see
presents in a pile,
Then I rip them all open
in a very short while.

Off into town with my
friends for a treat,
Shopping until we can't
feel our feet,
Stopping only to grab
something to eat.

Later that day is my
birthday tea,
Still knowing the day is all
about me,
Family and friends making it
as special as can be.

Hannah Power (12)
Bishop Ullathorne Catholic School, Coventry

Anthem For The Mosque At Ground Zero

I don't deny the broken families left behind that day,
Adoring parents weeping as the answering machine crackled with last goodbyes.
I don't deny the pinstripe suited, leather suitcased world
Turned upside down in a split second,
Water cooler nonchalance, clicking of computers
And 3,000 lifelines cut short by two winged shears.
And yet, as now, when right and left collide,
And Christian men and women bar the streets to tolerance and freedom,
As president to mayor, to senator,
Is chastised for open-mindedness
I ask, did not Aalim tell his wife not to worry
And to tell the kids he loved them
As John did?
Did not Tanisha,
Tears streaming down her cheeks as the planes loomed closer to the fibreglass brothers,
Tell her parents to live, live for her and not to cry
Or dwell on how she would have lived her life,
As Carole did?
And Daria and Lionel and Mahrus and Alex clasped hands and drew breath
Before glass flew and people fell and souls rose together, black, white,
Muslim, Christian, Hindu, Jew and Sikh,
Far from the pain their bodies had endured
To bliss and freedom, as millions mourned below,
And drew their own conclusions, spite breeding hate,
'They're from the same country, they're to blame!'
And the battle still rages, Christians to Muslims,
As Korans and bibles rise as smoke in the streets,
And far above, as victims look with shame on warring brothers,
And families protest against little Bashir and Zehna having a place to pray for Daddy to be safe up there,
Jesus, Mohammed wept.

Niamh Simpson (13)
Bryanston School, Blandford Forum

Once A Hater Of Life

Once a man hated music,
Even the ticking of his clock,
Even the word of this magic,
His life was simply in deadlock.

One night he fell asleep,
He normally dreamt of grey,
But suddenly in colour started to seep,
He started to run from the colour as if he was its prey.

He started to ask, 'Why is life against me?'
But a voice then responded, 'Because of your dark mind.'
'But I hate life, love and glee.'
'Change now or your death soon you'll find.'

The man then woke up with a start,
And began loving music with such passion.
So the more he listened, the bigger grew his heart,
He grew better at music and played it with compassion.

The more he played, the more he got famous,
He played even more until he could speak music,
Therefore more and more of this hole called darkness,
He is definitely enchanted by a spell of this magic.

Once a man loved music,
Even the ticking of his clock,
Even the word of this magic,
His life now isn't in deadlock.

Victor Vilela (13)
Burlington Danes Academy, London

Music And Me

The steady beat you see me nod my head to
Is the sound of my heart beating love for you.
I write the poem to something close to my heart
Music is my key, my end and start.

Abigail Asante
Burlington Danes Academy, London

I'm Happy To Be A Square

I'm a square, not a triangle,
I'm not that complicated.
I'm square, not a circle,
I've got friends by my side.
I'm a square, not a rectangle,
I'm not that tall.
I'm a square, not a pentagon,
I'm not that rich and stubborn.
I'm square, not an octagon,
My nickname is not octopus.
I'm a square, not a decagon,
I'm not that popular.
I'm a square and I'm proud to be.

Dami Aberuagba (12)
Buxton School, Leytonstone

No One Hears, No One Cares

I feel alone
I cry and cry
No one hears
No one cares
Each time I think
I'm all out of tears
Then I'm alone again

Is this depression
Or am I only just grieving?
I hope and pray
That someone will stop me breathing

The more I wait the more I cry
The more I hope
Someone will come
And embrace me and tell me
It's okay

I never feel loved
But I try and send it out
I don't even really know
What I'm sad about

Then I begin to hate
Myself
Just go out and smile
A smile is a subtle lie
To what's going on inside
Although sometimes it's not that easy to hide
Sometimes I just have to break out and cry

But still
No one hears
No one cares

I can't live by just facing my fears
The one thing I have, do and fear is my tears

Sometimes they help me
Sometimes they don't
I try and tell myself no!
Next time I won't

But next time I do
She says tears are good
I don't think that's true

Maybe she cries too
Maybe no one hears
But I definitely would care

Emotions are all we have
It's one thing we all share
Happy, sad, sane or mad
Rich, broke
Freezing cold or in a coat

Emotions show
Emotions grow
Let someone know
Let someone hear
Let someone care.

Parys Lanlehin Dobson (15)
Buxton School, Leytonstone

I'd Rather

I'd rather be silver than gold
I'd rather be quiet than bold

I'd rather live than die
I'd rather laugh than cry

I'd rather be good than bad
I'd rather be happy than sad

I'd rather be real than fake
I'd rather lie than snake

I'd rather remorse than regret
I'd rather recall than forget

I'd rather love than hate
I'd rather be early than late

I'd rather be together than alone
I'd rather stay out than go home

I'd rather watch than do
I'd rather be me than be you.

Dominique Joseph (13)
Buxton School, Leytonstone

What Matters To Me?

All the world's a landscape,
With all its ups and downs,
As the features of the land change.

The first age is the meadow,
Calm and peaceful with plants,
Creatures and birds that give this place its youth.

The next is the plain,
Ready to be shaped, it's a blank canvas,
And yet so full of ideas and dreams,
Hopes and desires, but too short to stay for long.

The hills, with their ups and downs,
Are teenagers with ever-changing theories,
Of where they are now and where they are to go.

Next the river, a torrent of ridiculed strength,
Its loud, outspoken ideas, fast to argue
And slow to back down and so this age flows
Into the next age.

The wise old oak forms the next stage,
Full of the past, never forgetting, withered
Yet withstanding the traits of old age.

The mountain, withered and weathered,
By the constant lashings of rain.
Drops of water washing away his youth.

As the mountains give way to hills
And plains, the man returns to his youth.
Finding himself in the place he was born.
The beginning and end of man in that special place,
Surrounded by plants, creatures and birds.

Matt Page (13)
Calday Grange Grammar School, West Kirby

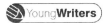

What Matters To Me

All the world's a theme park,
And all the boys and girls are the source of the jackpot:
And one man goes through many scenarios during his life,
His acts all come down to seven ages.
At first a staring toddler,
All happy and joyful going around and around under the security of Dad's arm.
Then a water ride,
Just bobbing up and down, cruising along the water's surface.
But that's just the beginning.
Then you enter a place where you are no longer in control,
The waves colliding left, right and centre,
Tossing its victim in all directions.
Then a small boy,
Being rejected everywhere he goes,
Gazing and staring at all the rides,
In disbelief and wonderment.
Then the world turns on its head,
Spinning around like you're on a roulette wheel,
Always wanting to go bigger and bigger.
Then it all gets too much to handle,
All the sugar and sweets then take their toll.
You fall to your knees and end up mewling and puking,
In a place you don't want to be seen.
Then, as you start to mature,
You start to get to know your limits.
Then you end up on the teacups again,
With your child
As they start their process
And you are coming to the end of yours.
Then you reach the end of the line,
Sitting on the sidelines,
Watching on.
You just have to sit there and watch others,
As they are taking part in what is known as,
Fun.

Charlie Quinn (14)
Calday Grange Grammar School, West Kirby

What Matters To Me

All the world's a theme park,
The ups and downs of life.
At first a baby mewling and
Non-stop crying just like the teacups.
Secondly, the child full of energy,
Restless bouncing into each other.
Reminds me of the bumper cars.
Growing up into a teenager,
The ups and downs of life.
One day happy and full of life,
The next a miserable, moody person.
The realisation of life,
It's not all good anymore.
This is like a roller coaster
With its ups and downs.
Then growing into a daring soldier,
Running into battle, full on contact.
Once you're there, you're there,
There's no going back from here.
This reminds me of a bungee jump.
Then growing into a dad,
Having to be caring and responsible,
Putting their lives before yours.
This reminds me of a simulator.
Then growing old into a grandad,
Not able to do much like you used to,
This reminds me of a Lazy River.
Then becoming half asleep,
Sans teeth, sans eyes, sans taste,
Sans everything.
This is just like a carousel,
Boring but peaceful.
All the world's a theme park,
The ups and downs of life.

Chris Marland (13)
Calday Grange Grammar School, West Kirby

What Matters To Me . . .

The world is a game
All the men and women are players
Games are full of fun, jokes and laughter
Games for children
Games for adults
Serious games
Enjoyment games
The anger and the joy all in one
Not always is the ending what you wished
But when it goes well
It can be life-changing
Every morning a new game begins
Some you will never want to forget
But others you would wish you could forget
Some romantic
Some not so nice.

Will O'Leary (13)
Calday Grange Grammar School, West Kirby

What Matters To Me

What matters to me is a theme park,
The sweet and sticky candyfloss fluttering in the breeze.
Fast roller coasters driving through the air, making everyone scream.
They throw their hands up in the air with excitement, giving them an
adrenaline rush.
Happy people rush and fuss over which ride they go on first.
They decide what the heck and run to the first one they see.
The big round teacups swirling round and round,
The children inside cower in fear or sit up, stare and cheer.

Daniel Ibrahim (13)
Calday Grange Grammar School, West Kirby

What Matters To Me

All the world's a jungle,
All the population just plants,
So many they all go unnoticed,
Just a colony of ants.

A new life starts in the jungle,
Just like it starts in our land,
A tiny seed lands in the soil,
Small enough to fit in your hand.

With water and sunlight the seed starts to grow,
Slowly but surely it grows,
The seed begins to sprout its leaves,
Sprouting into what? No one knows.

The weeks go by and leaves appear,
And slowly these leaves unravel,
But though the plant is getting quite tall,
In its life it has far to travel.

The leaves are wide, the stem is strong,
And now appears the bud,
But while the flower is growing on,
Trees around are chopped down for wood.

The bud is slowly opening,
Small petals revealing their colour,
Bright like a shining rainbow,
Glittering powder they are full of.

The flower as tall as it can be,
Towering above the grass blades,
Petals high above the ground they grow from,
To the worms goodbye it bades.

And now it's at its final stage,
It slowly withers away,
But as it dies a seed is dropped,
The plant is here to stay.

Luke Needham (13)
Calday Grange Grammar School, West Kirby

Holidays - My Whole Life's A Holiday

All the world is waiting,
Waiting for the next stage of life.
Just as the holiday is waited for.
You go on a holiday as soon as you can
And the seven stages of a holiday
Are the seven stages of man.

Booking the holiday,
Going through the many offers there happen to be.
You decide where to go
And when to go,
As you decide the name of your baby.

Preparing for the holiday,
Packing all your bags with stuff.
It's all so exciting, but it could all go wrong.
So many possibilities,
An infant at school.

Finally, the day has come.
The taxi draws up to your house at dawn.
You get in,
It goes,
It stops,
It goes,
It stops.
The journey to the airport.
The teenager's attitude.

Into the airport,
Onto the plane.
It revs up,
It growls,
It screams.
It runs at an unimaginable pace
And leaps into the air,
Over buildings, trees, cars and people.
It's so exciting.
Leaping into the unknown world of independence,
Becoming a man.

Arriving abroad in a foreign land,
The sun beating down like a hammer.
The kids, beaming like the sun
That's beating down like a hammer.
The staff smiling like the kids,
Who are beaming like the sun,
Which is beating down like a hammer.
Everything shining as you lie by the pool,
Everything calm, everything settled,
Everything happy in the house you live in.
The middle-aged man,
The happy man.

You have now retired,
Retired to your sun-lounger,
Lying comfortably,
The evening sun warming your tired body.
You've left the madness of the day,
You have retired from your job
And start to drift away.

The holiday is over,
Only memories are left,
Left of you.
Your time on this Earth has come to an end.

Joe McNeill (13)
Calday Grange Grammar School, West Kirby

Family

F amily are always there for you,
A nd they will always help you out.
M ums are there to look after you,
I n early and later life.
L et's remember this . . .
Y ou're lucky to have one.

I n some places people don't have them,
S ome people are orphans and don't have anyone who cares.

S ome have lost theirs to violence,
P eople cause war and murder,
E ating away people's lives.
C are for others
I n your own way,
A nd maybe they'll care for you.
L et's all remember this . . .

So treat yours well.

Adam Clift (12)
Calday Grange Grammar School, West Kirby

Know Your Friends

The music played loud, the sound of a tribe of warriors
Charging at you.
But the sound was the sound of memories, nice memories
And friendship cried out.
Whenever I won, lots of my friends were there with me.
They say when you lose, it doesn't matter,
But there's one thing that does matter, when you lose it,
That is friendship.

Jamie Duggan (12)
Calday Grange Grammar School, West Kirby

Human Rights

People have human rights,
But some don't understand.
The death penalty is ridiculous,
It's time to make a stand.

Rights are so important,
Especially the big one life
But some just go and ruin it
And stab you with a knife.

Respect each other's contributions,
Respect each other's rights,
But whatever you decide to do,
Don't go into the light.

James Martin (12)
Calday Grange Grammar School, West Kirby

Swimming

S wimming is amazing
W aterparks are fun
I like them outside
M ostly in the sun
M y mum swims a lot
I swim a lot
N early every day
G oing to the pool is the best thing that happens all day.

Alexander Craig (12)
Calday Grange Grammar School, West Kirby

War Poem

I was there
I saw everything
My life will never be the same

It all started in 1939
The war that changed my life
We went to Germany

It was night
No-man's land wasn't a quiet place
Bullets, grenades, anything that they could throw at us
Would fly over our heads

Every day, boom headshot
It was never the same
Not after October 19th 1940

We set out invading German lines
My friend Private Williams was on the frontline
Then a bullet sped through the air
Entered his head spreading blood everywhere

Too stunned to move
I stood there watching his body fall
Then all of a sudden, everything went black

I was dead.

Jacob Wright (12)
Calday Grange Grammar School, West Kirby

COD

COD6, COD6, COD6
It is not the Matrix
I shot you with my MP5
Don't care if you're dead or alive

COD5, COD5, COD5
Nazi zombies no one will survive
Damn, just got a teddy bear
No more magic weapon box to share

COD4, COD4, COD4
Golden eagles galore
Everyone thinks Price is dead
But he's held captive in a shed

COD3, COD3, COD3
Almost killed by a Nazi
The Japanese climb up a tree
That is how they surprise me

COD2, COD2, COD2
The graphics are really poo
You don't know what to do
And the Germans bomb you

COD1, COD1, COD1
I didn't know what went on
I'd rather eat a scone.

Matthew Clare (12)
Calday Grange Grammar School, West Kirby

Rugby

Crunching tackles, gruesome fights,
I do wonder is it worth getting hurt,
Just for that number 1 shirt?
Fans screaming, the rain is pouring,
But the rugby lads don't care,
Just as long as they win their share.

I could happily be at home watching Coronation Street,
But instead I'm playing rugby with my friend, Pete.
Bumps and bruises really hurt,
But it's worth it to wear that shirt,
With my good old friend, Curt.

To be part of the team, it feels great,
It's a good laugh and I have a good time,
I wish I was as good at rugby as I am at rhyme!

Jack Sanders (12)
Calday Grange Grammar School, West Kirby

My Childhood

What matters to me? A whole bunch of stuff,
But the most important is my childhood.
My first few years were a mess, but good,
Bing, bang, boom is what I can recall,
Throwing toys away and bumping into walls.
I just realised I've had a jolly good time.

The things that are so precious are my memories,
Merry, miserable and even confusing ones.
Without them I would only be a shell
With nobody I could tell.

Jonathan Tam (14)
Calday Grange Grammar School, West Kirby

Falling Into Light

The smell of sweat and fear
This fills the trench.
About half the men not older than 18
Take a toy too old for them.
A prayer is said by Company C
All I can see is me.
I look at my watch then my knee
It's 6.59am
I look away
For less than a day.
All of a sudden
A whistle blew
A man called 'Moooove!'
I pegged it to a groove
I climbed a ladder
Then boom!
My helmet fell
Blood I could tell
I fell to my knees
All I could see
Was a light coming to me
Then another
Boom!
A bullet hit me
The light jumped on me
It was over for me!

Robert Herbertson (12)
Calday Grange Grammar School, West Kirby

The Magic Of Reading

He was a pirate tasting the breeze,
He was on a ship sailing the seas,
He was an astronaut flying through space,
Then he was a driver in a race.

He was a soldier fighting in war,
Then he found a mysterious door,
He was on a submarine fighting the navy,
He was hungrily eating a bowl of gravy.

He was a wizard fighting Morgana Lefay,
They were lighting the sky that was grey,
He was a demi god son of Apollo,
He was chasing a car he needed to follow.

The magic of books was everywhere,
They capture you and take you there.

Danny Mabon (12)
Calday Grange Grammar School, West Kirby

Amazing Alliteration

M agic makes my mind mystified
A udience always acknowledge an amazing alliterative
   anthology matters to me most
T he thesaurus, 'tis terrific till used too much
T errible teachers try to terrorise terrific text, tut, tut, tut
E xcellent euphemism excites every examiner
R epetition, repetition, repetition, repeats rapidly, rhythmic
   but no rhyme
S in similes, sin similes . . . stop.

Joseph Schiller (13)
Calday Grange Grammar School, West Kirby

Weekend's Started

Weekend's started
School's departed
So I'm going home to get some rest
Long nights ahead
So time for bed
So that I can be the best

Saturday morning
Day is dawning
No time for breakfast, I've got to run
We have arrived at the market
We are in the car, so better park it
I'm more than sure this day will be fun

Nowhere else to roam
So we all return home
Finally I get to eat
But what to choose
Things to muse
I know, eggs, sausages and meat

Day goes on
Down goes sun
Time for bed I think
Can't wait till Sunday
But then there's Monday
I wish there wasn't that link

Sunday, roast day
Make the most day
But car boot first as normal
People's old treasure
Becomes my pleasure
But the roast is late, this is so tormental!

Now school's started
Weekend's departed
And all to do again next week.

Deane O'Shaughnessy (13)
Calday Grange Grammar School, West Kirby

The Rainforest

The rainforest is a vital issue,
And if it was destroyed
We will severely miss you.

The trees will die and I will try
Not to cry, as the lungs of
The world are destroyed.

Ruthlessly murdered
By a guy with a saw
The trees will live no more

Lots of people
Will lose their home
For a desperate attempt
To save what they own.

The land will be covered
By a stinking smoke
The yolk of the Earth
Has lost all hope.

So help us now
To save the forest
Do not ignore this
You are its only chance.

Joshua Sutton & Adam Clift (12)
Calday Grange Grammar School, West Kirby

Reading

You can read anywhere
On the couch, in bed
Even in your garden shed
Reading immerses you in a world
Of pirates and treasure, jewels and gold
Or a fantasy world of dwarves and elves
All these books on all those shelves
They can draw you into conspiracy
Or educate you on history
Hitler, Napoleon, queens, the Pope
And real-life stories of determined hope
From struggles to slaves
To mass murder graves
Anything you imagine
Everywhere you look
Can all be found
Inside a book.

George Kenny (12)
Calday Grange Grammar School, West Kirby

Fly

When I saw a bird in the sky,
I wondered why,
Is it because I am eating a pie
That I could not fly?

Harry Broadhurst (12)
Calday Grange Grammar School, West Kirby

I Love . . .

What matters to me
Is not what matters to you.
You may love your music,
Your family, your ambition,
I love achievin', getting far,
Enjoyin' life to the max.
Gotta keep pushin' forward,
Never lookin' back.
Reach for the stars
And never, never
Let anyone get in your way.

I love my family,
My friends, my sport,
But they can all wait
Until my goals are caught.

Will Broadbelt (13)
Calday Grange Grammar School, West Kirby

A Poem About Football

A football pitch is where I like to be
It is definitely the sport for me.
The feeling of scoring in a game
When the crowd is shouting your name

Although at times it doesn't go your way
It's all down to the way you play
If you want to get to the top of the game
You've got to work hard to get to fame

The football season is finally here
When men talk football as they drink their beer
I wonder who will win this year
I hope Liverpool's time is near.

Tom Cameron (11)
Calday Grange Grammar School, West Kirby

World Cup 2010

As South Africa hosts
For countries to play,
They put up the posts
To show them the way.

When linesmen shout
For offside calls,
Referees count
Goal-kick balls.

Jumping and shouting,
Getting dirty knees,
Scoring goals,
Goalkeepers saving penalties.

Vuvuzelas are blown
And puncture our hearing,
Players are on loan
And prices are dearing.

At last it comes to the match,
When players compete with others.
The time when players can snatch,
And families laugh at their brothers.

To move the ball across the ground
Requires a lot of skill,
To turn the ball and twist it around
Could make the score 1-0.

When yellow cards are given
And players start moaning,
Red cards are driven
And managers start groaning.

Paul Maddocks (12)
Calday Grange Grammar School, West Kirby

Winter

Crisp autumn leaves hardened by frost,
Drop to the ground and summer is lost.

As the first snow falls and whitens the river,
The bare trees shiver.

Snow crunches beneath my feet,
Layers of crisp, white sheets.

Children sleep, restless through the night,
And wake to windows silvery white.

Icy men are made with sightless eyes,
A crisp carrot from Mum and one of Dad's ties.

At the end of the day the kids retire,
And drink hot chocolate in front of the fire.

George Tipton (11)
Calday Grange Grammar School, West Kirby

I'd Be Canadian

On a sidewalk under the trees,
I walk on a floor of maple leaves.

Surrounded by the colours of orange and red,
From the street,
Beneath my feet,
To the sky above my head.

I love it all from the east to the west,
It's the country where I relax best.

Summers of sunshine,
Winters of snow,
All year round it's a great place to go.

If I could choose
Where else to be from,
There's no question I'd
Be Canadian.

Nathan Kellner (13)
Calday Grange Grammar School, West Kirby

What Matters To Me

What matters to me is . . . um, I dunno,
Maybe it's the rain or the sun or the snow.
No, it's the ball from the Liverpool match,
Or my home, sometimes we call it the hatch.
Oh, of course it's my family
And all of my friends,
But not Harry Hall, he drives me round the bend.
I also like happiness
And obviously world peace,
And football,
And money,
And a holiday to Greece.
And . . . well . . . that's about it,
I can't think of any more,
Except Everton, friendship and definitely no war.

Daniel Atherton (13)
Calday Grange Grammar School, West Kirby

Red

Ravishing rude to changing mood
Who'd have thought of this for red.
Maybe outside or in a bed.
But that's not for me, for me is red,
The way it is so angry, yet so elegant.
It shows the anger in the morning,
That's why it's the colour of warning,
In the night it is such a delight
To see red in the sky so alight.
The colour of love and the blood of a dove,
But what matters about red is the way it is said,
Red, red, red, it can show the dead,
But that's not why it matters to me,
It matters because of its personality.

Maxwell Shaw (13)
Calday Grange Grammar School, West Kirby

All Mixed Up!

A pencil is a piece of lead,
Embraced with wood like a lover
Covering his cold girl with the warmth of his coat,
So stiff with strength and so soft with love.
Oh no!
What was the topic?
Was it 'what matters to me'?
Oh, let's see . . .
Hmm . . .
Aah, the train,
It was a major breakthrough,
It was worked by steam,
Ha, ha!
Just like the lid on Tom's head blows open,
When he gets angry with Jerry.
It moves on rails,
On a fixed path,
Like a hypnotised man.
No! No! No!
Urghhh!
Not trains!
That does not matter to me.
Let's see!
The moon landing.
The greatest thing ever, to mankind.
No! No! That's not it!
Aah! I've got it now.
For sure.
Cooking! Ya, that's what matters to me, 'cooking'.

No! No!
Urgh!
I'm just a confused young man!

Kurush Medhora (13)
Calday Grange Grammar School, West Kirby

What I Want But What I'll Get

You ask what I would most want to be
What matters to me? Why don't you see?
I'm quite fond of the sky above
To flutter about and be like a dove
Oh, how it has been my dreams
But that won't happen, without wings it seems
I could grow a pair if I ate feathers
They'd need a boil with spikes like heathers
But to see all the land directly below
How tourists would pay to see such a show
All fluffy and white my body would look
Although I hope I don't end up meal of the cook
Well, I don't think this will happen in my life
I'll probably have children, a dog and a wife.

Well, I'll see you on Thursday to write again
So fingers crossed it doesn't rain.

Harry Hall (13)
Calday Grange Grammar School, West Kirby

The Chilean Miner Rescue

They would rather be above than under,
In the darkness they did wonder,
If they'd ever see the light of day,
All they could do was sit there and pray.

Down under they were stuck,
Until a bit of luck!
One man thought of a plan,
To rescue every single man,
Because others didn't know what to do,
They invented the phoenix two.

'Viva Chile!' the crowd screamed and waved,
As all thirty-three miners were successfully saved.

Ben Acton (12)
Calday Grange Grammar School, West Kirby

Peace

Peace is what the world needs
It whispers through tall trees
Without it life just cripples
And death simply ripples
The army would be abolished
They would have no more shoes to polish
All the lives that were wasted
May never have tasted
Life without war or murder
Because in life they may have got further
Than pulling the trigger of a gun
When they could have been having more fun.

Alexander Youngson (11)
Calday Grange Grammar School, West Kirby

My Letter To You

Dear Poetry Matters,
I have something to say,
I'm writing a poem,
I'll send it today.

Be sure to read it,
It will blow your mind,
It's a letter that I write.

You'll receive it by night,
You'll read it by day,
You may like it and tell me
And I'll jump and say, 'Hooray!'

Letters matter to me,
They help me make my point,
Just to show whoever reads,
That I took my time to write.

Jack Turner (13)
Calday Grange Grammar School, West Kirby

Alright?

Alright?
Good,
Cos you're in for a fright.
What matters to me?
Let's find out . . .

My family of course,
That's everyone's thought,
They make you do chores,
But you adore them.

Hmmm . . . let's see,
Brazil, that's a good un,
That country, that capital B,
My home town.

Next, my future,
Fun, forced and fought for,
Jobs in life, like law,
A must for us.

Man United,
What a team.
It loves to win trophies,
It's like a drug to me!

What else? Me mates,
Yeah, that sounds good.
Have fun in Liverpool,
Make my mum broke!

Nearly near the end,
Holidays to relax,
To get tans,
To get texts,
Sayin' 'I'm jealous.'

Last but not least,
A question for yous,
What matters to you?
You bunch of fools!

Felipe Pacheco (13)
Calday Grange Grammar School, West Kirby

Shoes

You know what I think?
I think you can tell a lot about a person
Just from their shoes.
Feeling good?
Feeling bad?
What's the news?
It's amazing the inspiration that's around,
Amazing and blazing, just waiting to be found.
Look at that posh bloke with the briefcase
And the perfect, polished, pristine leather loafers.
Look at his smile, such style, meanwhile
There's the tramp in the corner,
With the ripped up shirt,
Wearing those skanky, manky boots covered in dirt.
What about that jogger,
Running past fast?
See those new, sleek trainers, that arrived at last.
But I'm really drawn to that kid over there,
Out with his mates with the strangely cut hair.
Look at those luminous things on his feet,
People stop and stare as they light up the street.
Those weird, bright laces, causing startled faces,
That's the kind of shoe I want,
Making people stop and say, 'Wow!'
I'm going to have those shoes,
Someway,
Somehow.

Michael Simpson (13)
Calday Grange Grammar School, West Kirby

Music

What matters to me,
Like 1, 2, 3,
Is the beat, the sound, the melody.
Cos music is here and music is now,
I listen, I like, I play it loud.
Dubstep to rap, I hear them all,
From electro to trance, I hear them call.
I pick it out,
I choose it fast,
I make sure
The rhythm lasts.
It makes me sing,
It makes me dance,
It puts me in a magic trance.
I hear the sound,
I hear the beat,
It makes me get
Up on my feet.

Matthew Hale (13)
Calday Grange Grammar School, West Kirby

Chips

I like chips
They are very tasty on my lips
Especially with some spicy dips
They go very well with crunchy chips
Chips are so greasy and fatty
That just makes me a lot more chatty
When they are salty
They will not be faulty
It shall go well with fish
On a large dish
I like chips
They are very tasty on my lips.

Harry Das (11)
Calday Grange Grammar School, West Kirby

What Matters To Me

Swimming is what matters to me,
When I'm in the water I feel so free,
The 2012 Olympics must be for me,
That gold medal will be mine, you just wait and see.

Breaststroke, back, fly or free,
Whatever the stroke it doesn't bother me.
Breaststroke stands out from the other three,
On that podium I will be.

The training becomes hard when you reach level 3,
My muscles ache head to knee,
But I know where I will be,
Olympic swimmer, that will be me!

Alexander Congdon (11)
Calday Grange Grammar School, West Kirby

It Happened To Me

Last year I had a cat,
And what mattered to me was my cat.
Although I loved him, I needed to get away,
Cos of all the pain and holes in the mat.
This makes me think of him more today.
He scavenged for food,
Put my dad in a mood,
I mean even one night he was causin' a fight.
Then one fateful day,
I was walkin' away,
I got a call from my dad,
He said it was bad . . .
The
Cat
Is
Dead.
Do you know how it feels
To have someone you love
Taken out by some wheels
To see them white as a dove?

Aidan Dunn (13)
Calday Grange Grammar School, West Kirby

Volcanoes Matter!

What matters to me is volcanoes,
The things that created our planet,
With one bang it could kill thousands,
Yet at the same time, without them,
I wouldn't be here writin' this,
You wouldn't either.
Nobody would.
They made us.

Without them we wouldn't have Iceland or Hawaii,
And imagine a world without Hawaii, hey,
Exactly.

Without volcanoes the Earth would explode,
All the heat inside wouldn't be able to escape
And before you knew it,
Boom!
And we're all gone.

Without volcanoes we'd have no atmosphere,
No life,
No death,
No nothin',
Just another ball of rock in space.

So what d'you think?
Friend or foe?
Good or bad?
Creators or destroyers?
It's your choice . . .

Luke Williams (14)
Calday Grange Grammar School, West Kirby

The Five Disciplines Of Rugby

What matters to me, probably won't matter to you.
Rugby is what matters to me personally.

A hard hitting,
Fast flowing,
Super fun,
Man's game.

Rugby matters to me because it builds respect,
It brings sportsmanship to a rough game.

A hard hitting,
Fast flowing,
Super fun,
Man's game.

In this game you will really need discipline,
Enjoyment means you will not get bored.

A hard hitting,
Fast flowing,
Super fun,
Man's game.

You will learn to use teamwork,
These are the five disciplines of rugby.

Michael Pritchard-Howarth [13]
Calday Grange Grammar School, West Kirby

The Power Of Music

What matters to me is music
It twists and turns and shapes the way we feel
It creates an image that can be ideal
To anyone listening to a brilliant piece
When they sit down, relax and let their emotions release
Into a fuzz of thoughts, memories and feelings
Which can be to someone extremely appealing
If they're stressed, troubled, happy or in love
Music comes along and gives 'em a shove and says
'Hey, don't worry, music has come'
Look up to the sky and see the sun
Listen up closely if you think you're a lover
Music's how countries confer with each other
By sharing cultures, communities and being kind
Come join us and leave all that war and hatred behind
Lightening the mood with music ain't wrong
So let's come together and all praise the song
It's better than religion where everyone just can't decide
With music it's easy to find your emotions inside
We don't need to speak the same language or have the same time
We can all understand each other by playing in rhyme
Music is everywhere, as far as you can see
And that's why music is what matters to me.

Dom Mazhindu (13)
Calday Grange Grammar School, West Kirby

What Matters To Me Is That It Shall Never End

Sometimes life can be happy,
Sometimes life can be sad,
Sometimes people are happy,
Sometimes people are sad.
Sometimes you feel like everything has gone wrong,
And you have reasons to be sad,
And sometimes you feel that everything goes right -
For some people.
What haven't I done?
What have I done?
Do they deserve this?
Or am I a sinner for being jealous?

Things start and things stop,
When people believe things carry on,
No matter what happens,
We *have* to breathe to live,
But we *choose* to live,
So live right and spread goodness.
No matter what happens,
It shall never end.

Rafael Cavallini (13)
Calday Grange Grammar School, West Kirby

What Matters To Me

All the world's a library,
When you and everyone else is a book,
And all the books have different readers.
At first there is the new release, a book is born!
And there's a big commotion made of you.
Then promotion day,
A glamorous premiere of entrancing dresses, and people,
When also you are published into the scary world
Of schools and homes.
Then the lover, when all the girls scream for you
Because you achieved an award for being, well, good!
Then the soldier, when you fight to be best-seller
And all your needs are stretched.
Then when the book gets justice,
When awarded and sold steadily,
And you realise all is good.
Then when you become a classic,
The girls that screamed for you then,
Read it to their children and it is a
Loved family novel.
Then to be an elder and you need help
To keep up your sales, but no one really makes
A fuss of you, no glory, no awards,
No nothing.

Audley Cruttenden (14)
Calday Grange Grammar School, West Kirby

What Matters To Me

All of the world's a forest
All the people, little animals
Their whole life is like a creature

The baby is a tiny mouse
Curled up in its mother's nest
Sleeping, sleeping, and when it wakes
Calling for its mother's arms.

After that, the child's a rabbit
Prancing around, playing
With its friends and siblings
Fleeing at signs of danger.

The teen is a singing bird
Impressing lovers with its voice
Slightest thing makes it burst into song
Angered easily, storms back to its nest.

The young man is a ferret
Searching the forest floor for food
Left by parents to fend for itself
Thinking of starting a new family.

As he gets older, he is an owl
A father of a family
Hunting for food for his young
Wise, and breaks up the arguments.

As middle age comes, he is a fox
Ready for anything
Clever and sly
Finding food after his young have left

Finally, a badger
Greying hair and muzzle
Tires easily, rests in his den
Crippled legs cannot carry his body.

Jacob Swan (13)
Calday Grange Grammar School, West Kirby

All The World's A Race: What Matters To Me

All the world's a race,
A race to live, a race not to die.
At first the start,
The tension, the waiting for the whistle to blow,
The race to start, the wrestle to end.
Next the sprint, the way to run
Away, away from the massive crowd,
Coming close, too close!
Then muscles tiring, every step hurts,
Pain like fire, sharp pain!
Now the numb feeling,
All I think:
Up, forward, down,
To keep your feet running,
Running towards the finish line.
Vaguely noticing the crowd,
Cheering, shouting, running
After me, but everything
I notice, is the finishing line.
The finishing sprint,
To end the race,
To win the trophy.
Faster, faster, faster,
But too slow?
No!
The trophy is won,
The race is finished,
But everything I want
Is to be down and to sleep
Because I'm tired,
Tired, tired, tired,
Too tired!

David Eckl [13]
Calday Grange Grammar School, West Kirby

Me Life

I like football,
I like sport,
I like being cheeky,
But without getting caught.

I love swimming,
But would rather do hockey,
If I chose to play rugby,
I'd have to be stocky.

Me, I love my family,
With Tiegan, Nell and Ben,
I also love writing stories,
Especially in pen.

All me bros and sisters,
They get into bed,
But early in the morning,
They're jumpin' on me head.

When you play footie,
You should always get the ball,
But when you play rugby,
There's always blood and gore.

Jake Mathot (11)
Calday Grange Grammar School, West Kirby

Dreams

Every day when I go to bed, something roams around my head
Sometimes, I'm a bird soaring in the bright blue sky
Sometimes, I'm a mosquito drinking some sweet blood
Sometimes, I'm a fish swimming through the seaweed

Every day when I go to bed, something roams around my head
Sometimes, I'm a tree blowing in the autumn wind
Sometimes, I'm a flower, insects are invading me
Sometimes, I'm a rock, you really cannot break me

Every day when I go to bed, something roams around my head
Sometimes, I'm on the run in a Lamborghini with police on my tail
Sometimes, I'm a proper winner having all that I want
Sometimes, I'm a loser having a very miserable life.

Every day when I go to bed, something roams around my head
Sometimes, I'm Superman beating up the bad guy
Sometimes, I'm Spider-Man swinging from web to web
Sometimes, I'm Batman having a black cape
But suddenly, everything turns normal.

Shasank Loharuka (11)
Calday Grange Grammar School, West Kirby

Life

Life is a magnificent thing
A thing that should be looked after and treated in all the right ways
A thing that is a dream and you can be a success
A thing that is a challenge or puzzle for you to adventure with
A thing that gives many opportunities that you can experiment with
A thing that is a reality and is yours to keep
A thing that can be sorrow that can break your heart
A thing that is dreadful that can make life fall apart
A thing that is happy and should be kept that way
A thing that can be confusing but you will learn
A thing that is a balance and can change at any time
A thing that conceals all your hopes and dreams
A thing that is an explosion where something awful or nice can happen
A thing to be cherished and kept in good hands
A thing that is precious and shouldn't be destroyed
A thing that keeps on going
A thing that goes on forever.

Ben Hamlett (11)
Calday Grange Grammar School, West Kirby

Everton FC

'Come on you Blues!' the crowd all roar,
Cahill's the best, he's bound to score.

Fellaini jumps in the air,
The other players he's going to scare.

Baines is running up the wing,
'Cross it in!' the crowd all sing.

Go, go Baines, cross he will,
What a header, that goal was brill.

Amazing goal, now that's two nil,
Soon enough the time must fill.

They get a break, he shoots from far,
But Howard punches it off the bar.

The whistle signals the end of the game,
Everton have won again.

Robert Love (12)
Calday Grange Grammar School, West Kirby

Sports Stars

Lewis Hamilton is the best
Better than all the rest
Rooney is proud of wearing the crest
Usain Bolt does not have a test

Ali was the bees' knees
Ian Poulter hits it off tees
Tom Watson comes in with knees
Nigel De Jong has had a lot of fees

Amy Williams was a star
She was quicker than a racing car
Pele was better than Louis Saha
Tiger Woods can hit it far

Michael Jordan is so tall
Amir Khan will never fall
Roger Federer can't half hit a ball
Phil Taylor has never thrown in a wall.

Conor Clements (12)
Calday Grange Grammar School, West Kirby

What Matters To Me

In my life I like to play
Many sports to fill my day.
Football, rugby, running too,
To sport I'm addicted, it's true!

My family time is full of fun,
Not only holidays in the sun.
Scuba diving, fishing trips -
It's hard to choose my favourite bits.

My brother Jack can be a pain
And often drives me quite insane.
But having him as my brother,
He is a mate like no other.

My mum and dad tend to nag,
They constantly say I should be glad!
I know they care and are not too bad
But boy, I wish I had a gag.

My relatives are really cool,
My Uncle Mark works in football.
My Grandma is really quaint
And Grandpa teaches me how to paint.

My life is great, I have a ball,
My friends are tops and the best of all!
This sums up my life so far,
Can't wait for the next bit. Ta-ta!

Will Gibson (11)
Calday Grange Grammar School, West Kirby

Spike

Spike is the name of my rabbit,
He has a very bad habit
Of clawing and scratchin'
When you try and catch 'im,
But if you give him some mint,
He will nab it.

I have a young rabbit called Spike,
Who I took for a ride on my bike.
He flew off the back,
And as a result of that,
I no longer have a rabbit called Spike.

What happened to my rabbit, Spikey?
I think it is more than likely
That he got on the train
And travelled to Spain,
To look for his lost cousin, Mikey.
    Olé!

Miles Knoop (11)
Calday Grange Grammar School, West Kirby

The Trees!

It is a windy day here today
Where the trees like to wave
And want to show off their beautiful greenness
People climb them, for enjoyment.

People cut them down to make money
And people lean on them
But the trees are not finding this fun.

We say that there are plenty more trees
Left in the world,
But if we keep cutting them down,
We are virtually killing the world and us.

If the trees could talk,
They would have a voice to be heard,
But they cannot talk,
So people think it is fine to climb them and cut them,
But it is not.
Help the trees. Save yourself.

Oliver Kelly (13)
Calday Grange Grammar School, West Kirby

A Pilot

I want to be a pilot
Not so much a pirate
The RAF is for me
Not so much the army
I've just finished my mission
Good thing I ran out of ammunition
To feel free and alive in the sky
I'm nothing like stir-fry
I'd rather be in the cockpit
The feeling is quite summat
I have been promoted a rank
For destroying a German tank
I'm now a Lt Col
My navigator is sassy and has a journal
They say to me, 'Hello, sir'
I say, 'Go and cut your hair'
My favourite is a dogfight
Just not in the middle of the night
Damn it, they shot my mullet
I was just killed by a bullet.

Lee Churchill (12)
Calday Grange Grammar School, West Kirby

Pilot

I want to be a pilot
Not so much a pirate
To fly so high
Saying bye-bye
To those on the ground
Which are already specks on the mound

I want to be a pilot
In the RAF
Going up the ranks
By shooting tanks.

Jack Leary (12)
Calday Grange Grammar School, West Kirby

Luxurious Chocolate

The supple chocolate disintegrated
As it hit my teeth,
It was delightful.
I thought about letting it
Dissolve onto my tongue.

The aroma was so luxurious and rich,
I thought if I hadn't taken a tiny morsel,
I would have died by torture!

Tension was high,
It was so mouth-watering,
I was tempted.
I had to take another bite
And I did.
It was delicious,
It was like I had died and gone to Heaven.

Daniel Francis (13)
Edmonton County School, London

Scrumptious Chocolate

Tantalisation,
As I looked at the chocolate,
Like slithering silver it slid slowly
Down my mouth,
As it jumped out the wrapper,
As shiny as the sea,
I can hear the crispy, crackling noise
From the wrapper,
As I scoffed it like a pig,
I watched everyone eat theirs,
I was devastated.

Janan Kolcak (13)
Edmonton County School, London

Dairy Milk

As I gazed at the chocolate,
It cried, 'Eat me, I'm irresistible!'
I put the delicious chocolate in my mouth,
It started to melt, it was like being in Heaven!
I could feel the chocolate move around my mouth
As I could smell the chocolate.
It was like the smell climbed to my nose,
As if I could smell something sweet and succulent.

Kayleigh Small (13)
Edmonton County School, London

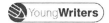

Mason

(In loving memory of Mason O'Neil Springer, RIP)

You were my friend, but you were like a brother,
    I never met anyone like you, you were like no other.
My heart was wrenched out once you were gone,
    Everything else seemed to go wrong.

You were a bright soul that lit up my life,
It was like my heart had been twisted with a knife.

You were so mad, but you made me laugh,
    When you left, my heart was broken in half.
You were everything to me,
    And I hope you did see,
Just how amazing you are,
    You were our beautiful star.

You were
A bright soul who
Lit up my life, it was like
My heart had been
Twisted with
A knife . . .
Even though I miss you, I have to understand,
God took you for a reason
To help protect
The land,
To help protect me,
And your family,
Even though we're apart,
I haven't
Lost you, 'cause you're still in my
Heart . . .
You were a bright soul who lit up my life,
It was like my heart had been twisted with a knife,
But I will see you again,
When it's my time,

Until then I know you will be fine,
So this is my way of saying goodbye,
        We may have lost an angel,
But Heaven has *gained* one.

Jasmine Eames (13)
Edmonton County School, London

My Extraordinary Mother

My mum is a precious gem to me,
You can tell that by her golden beauty.
Everyone would mistake her for a diamond goddess,
She would wear a light, frothy, ivory-white dress.
She is technically powerful and filled with stealth,
You would buy a candle and light up her health.

My mum is so good to me,
Her anger is the size of a pea.
My mum plays with me all the time,
And sets off the birds' cheerful chime.

Through the oblivion,
Scrolling through the past,
She sets her eyes on you
And oh, they're so vast.

Let bluebells be whisked away
And tomorrow be a fresh new day.
Her bubbling cauldron could not be shy,
Let your moist tippy-toes touch the sky.

Joe Benjamin Dwerryhouse (11)
Eggbuckland Community College, Plymouth

Fashion

Fashion is important to me,
Yet I really don't know why,
If Daddy won't buy me those shoes,
I might start to cry.
Mummy says, 'Those heels are too high.'
Then my daddy argued that it will make me less shy.

My favourite shop is called New Look
And maybe Primark too.
But never wear your new shoes
To the animal zoo.
There are lots of fashionable people in my street,
Yet everyone likes my shoes,
They look at my feet.
Heels, heels, I love you,
All I want is Jimmy Choo's.

You matter to me, I will tell you why,
When I don't wear them I feel I will die.

My face smiles whenever I see those boots,
In my brain it always computes
That they are my favourites,
But more are to be,
I love them all, hee-hee.

If I break a heel I feel I will faint,
And I will make a serious complaint.
Sometimes people get me all wrong,
Just because I like fashion,
Doesn't mean I'm a dumb blonde.

Tolon Andrews (11)
Eggbuckland Community College, Plymouth

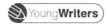

Great Expectations

Great Expectations
Oh Great Expectations
What a joy you are to read

From the tiny little forge and house
To a great extension
With a great helping hand

From being bullied and stared at
To his generous luck
And his brutal sister
A little luck makes a difference

I would like to try and find out
What happens next
Is anyone's guess
So I'd better read it
Till I find out

With a list of great expectations
Which can only be carried out
By a great gentleman
Which is young Pip

I like reading very much
But this is my favourite book
For a whole list of reasons
Which none can compare.

Christopher Smith (11)
Eggbuckland Community College, Plymouth

TV Sonnet

Person:
The flashing colours of TV are bright,
I love to watch you every single day,
And every time I'm with you, I feel right.
I remember the month I bought you - May.

TV:
I feel tired, you watch me every day!
I go mad when you change the channel.
'The weather is cloudy today,' they say.
In the news there was fire in the Tunnel.

Person:
But without you, I've got nothing to do,
You're the radio and the light in my room.
I would be bored and alone without you
And all the good programmes start after noon.

TV:
I'm really tired, I work day and night,
So please! Leave me alone, just for tonight!

Margarita Tolstaya (13)
Glenmoor School for Girls, Bournemouth

Your Smile

Your smile is infectious,
I think of it day and night.
When you smile, I smile,
Anything to catch your sight.

Your smile is all I dream,
I long to look in your eyes.
When you smile, I smile,
And I don't have to hide.

Your smile gives me butterflies,
A feeling I can't explain.
When you smile, I smile,
It's driving me insane.

Your smile makes me faint,
You really touch my heart.
When you smile, I smile,
You're my shining star.

Your smile allows me to fall in love,
And I don't know how.
When you smile, I smile,
I'm on a higher ground.

Your smile makes me go crazy,
My worries disappear.
When you smile, I smile,
I really need you here.

Your smile is all I need
And I know this for a fact.
Because whenever you smile at me,
I make sure that I'm smiling back.

Tia Wells (13)
Glenmoor School for Girls, Bournemouth

Feelings In Ruby Tanya

(Inspired by 'Ruby Tanya' by Robert Swindells)

My name is Ruby Tanya,
Today a bomb blew up my school.
My dad says it's the asylum seekers' fault.
I know he's wrong.
My best friend, Asra, is one of them,
But he doesn't know.

My name is Asra,
Today a bomb blew up my school.
People are saying we are terrorists,
But we know we didn't do it.
My best friend is Ruby Tanya,
I hope she still wants to be my friend.

Ruby Tanya is my daughter,
Today a bomb blew up her school.
It's those stupid asylum seekers' fault,
I'm going to do something about it -
Put up posters all around Tipton Lacey,
Lamp the Camp, that's what they are going to say.

Hillery Phillip (12)
Hillcrest School, Birmingham

School's Been Bombed

A building bombed from far away,
Asylum seekers have gone away.

One person killed, two people hurt,
The person killed was called Bert.

Police cover the school,
While kids play ball.

Police try and find the guilty one,
While more try and find another bomb.

A building bombed from far away,
Asylum seekers have gone away.

Jade Loxton (12)
Hillcrest School, Birmingham

Ruby Tanya

(Inspired by 'Ruby Tanya' by Robert Swindells)

Ruby Tanya is my name
And my friend, Asra, who one day came.
She was an asylum seeker and got blamed,
Even my dad said they should be ashamed.

My dad is very patriotic,
If he found out I was Asra's friend, everything would be chaotic.
All the asylum seekers are in trouble,
And all their problems are double.

Dad was handing out leaflets, which gave me a bad feeling,
I knew straight away with what Dad was dealing.
All I knew was that Dad was up to no good,
But I never understood
Why he hated the asylum seekers so much.

Patricia Tamayem (12)
Hillcrest School, Birmingham

The Ocean

The waves are as smooth as sand, not being wild
The ships' bells are silent like a mouse
The flags are high and proud, like a child going to school
The wind is swaying in the air, silent, but not still
The shore is safe, homey as can be
The ocean is alive, full with grace and glee.

Jasmine Pandit (11)
Hitchin Girls' School, Hitchin

My Little Sisters

My hairband's gone,
My brush nowhere,
My sisters get in everywhere.
Through my stuff,
They hunt and search,
They drive me totally berserk.

But at night when it is dark,
Tucked up in bed,
They look so small,
Not the menaces I think at all.
I kiss goodnight,
They look and smile,
My sisters are peaceful for a while.

Morning comes, they're wide awake,
I tell them to hurry or we will be late.
They make the toast,
I make the tea,
We're such a team, my sisters and me.

Hannah Malyon (13)
Hitchin Girls' School, Hitchin

Dreams Of A Very Special Cat

The day is here
The night is gone
The dawn has passed
We still go on
The glistening stars
Look down and find
That all of Earth
Is here to stay
And me and Angus
My slinki Malinki
Look up to the stars
And think it's so pretty
I dream of them too
And sometimes I dream that
Angus my cat
Is on the moon
The moon glides round
Our little home
And watches us
Forlorn, alone
And as we all sleep
We like to keep
A golden locket
In our minds
Of our dreams
We keep them discreet
So no one will see
But I'll tell you something
It's very special to me
It keeps me safe
And snuggled up
Like a soft blanket
Like a warm hug
So you see
This is why my dreams
Are special
And keep me snuggled
This is why

My dreams keep me safe
Because my cat
My slinki Malinki
My very special cat, Angus
Is in them all.

Shamma Dalal (13)
Hitchin Girls' School, Hitchin

How Far Would You Go - The Effects Of Pollution

How far would you go to kill a living thing?
Would you kill a bird who's only joy was to sing?
How far would you go to make the world die fast?
Could you release the evil used so much in the past?

How far would you go to let trees and plants die?
Would you slaughter a tree when its only goal was to grow so high?
How far would you go to help our death?
Could you kill someone by yourself by polluting their breath?

How far would you go to make the blue skies turn grey?
Could you make it so your child would never see the light of day?
How far would you go to stop a cat saying miaow?
Well, it's time to wake up because it's happening now.

Yasmin Gariba-Hamilton (11)
Hitchin Girls' School, Hitchin

My Mum

My mum is the only one who matters to me.
I love her dearly and she loves me.
She treats me well and makes me happy,
She stays with me through thick and thin
And always tells me it will be okay.
She's the only one who truly matters to me,
When I'm disappointed and I start crying,
She hugs me and comforts me
And gives me cups of tea.
My mum's the only one who matters to me,
I love her like there's no tomorrow.
She hugs me when I graze my knee,
I love my mum and she loves me.
She's the only one I love.

Sophie Harris (11)
Hitchin Girls' School, Hitchin

No Bullying

(I wrote about this because I think bullying should be stopped)

They cause me sleepless nights,
I go to school in fear,
They cause me so much pain,
I want to end it here.

I'm anxious as well as terrified,
Of what they're gonna do,
They make me feel friendless,
How would you feel if it was you?

I feel as small as a mouse,
I shiver in fear inside,
They're gonna get me after school,
I know I'll try and hide.

They kick me, hit me and punch me,
As well as hurting me inside,
Mum asked me about my bruises,
And every time I lied.

Abbie Clarke (11)
Hitchin Girls' School, Hitchin

Thinking

i think
and I think
and start to think
that thinking spawns
think, and after thinking
too much, the think starts to
become a void word, because
the think is thought about for too
long, and now it is just a little think
stamped in black and white on a page
of think.

Millie Morris (16)
Hitchin Girls' School, Hitchin

Watcher

The moonlit night,
That shone so bright,
Wistful eyes gazing down,
Watching those glued to the ground,
Undisturbed by midnight clouds,
Incomplete, always, and never full,
Paradox of its universe,
Harsh, unforgiving, dreadful curse,
Scanned by many rarely touched,
Over centuries has become too much,
Sadness etched deep as scars,
In that face just like ours,
Spare a thought for those above,
White and pale as the peaceful dove,
Gaze upon it in silent awe,
Memories of those lost in forgotten wars,
Do not forget,
All that it has met with watchful eyes,
Emotions that it cunningly hides,
As dawn approaches, loosen your hold,
Shine your light upon a different world.

Amy Saunders (16)
Hitchin Girls' School, Hitchin

The Sky's Reflection

Mother of pearl,
Like something out of this world.
Indigo and violets,
Moving quickly like fighter pilots.
Pink blossom and red rose,
Every colour created goes.
Blues and aquamarines,
Secret treasure always gleams.
More beautiful than the aurora,
Because it's so much purer.
Like a perfect picture painting,
But humanity is tainting.
Because of our nature of destruction,
We will never save the sky's reflection.

Imogen Richardson (14)
Hitchin Girls' School, Hitchin

What Matters?

What matters to you,
So far on high?
Do you really care
When people die?

Or are we just your playthings?
Little ants to crush at will.

What matters to you,
So far below?
Do you cry
When it's someone's time to go?

And are you ashamed when people kill
The innocent for fun?

What matters to us,
Stuck in-between?
With our fear of Heaven,
But what does that mean?

Does it mean that we are free?
Or does it crowd what we can see?
Can religion light the path?
Or merely ignite our human wrath?

Josie Thomas (14)
Hitchin Girls' School, Hitchin

The Town Crier

The town crier, the town crier
Why are you such a liar?
No one should trust him
He is so thin
The town crier, the town crier
Oh, why are you such a liar?
Everything that he has ever said
Was a little lie
But his ties are all the same.

Samantha Rawlings (11)
Hitchin Girls' School, Hitchin

Living The Wars

War started centuries ago.
By the looks of the current situation, it will never stop.
People die in wars, little children and their families die.
They can't do anything except wait and cry.

The people who are stuck in the middle of the war
Don't watch TV or listen to songs,
All they do is sit and hear bangs from the outside
And listen to the planes which are dropping the bombs.

The other things they listen to are loud thuds and bangs on the door.
It's not a strong door, it's only big, old, brown wood
And after a few kicks from the strong soldier, the door's on the floor.

From the outside, people see a flash and hear a couple of shouts,
But inside it's a blood bath.
Parents shot in the back and chest
And children shot in the head while they were sleeping in bed.

All this was once Germany, Vietnam, Iraq and Afghanistan.
I have to stop here because the list is too long.

Ghazi Ali (15)
Hodge Hill School, Birmingham

What Matters To Me Are my Pets!

My cute cat
My devilish dog
My charismatic chicken
My friendly fish
My gorgeous guinea pig
My rapid rabbit
My talkative tortoise
My perilous pony
My handy hamster
My gentle gerbil
My house is like a zoo!

Cecily Cullen (11)
Holbrook High School, Ipswich

What Matters To Me

What matters to me is my family,
My family is what matters to me.

Not just the humans, but the pets too,
They act just like us, but are cuter than you.

My raging rabbit that wants to break free,
My goldfish, my goldfish that is older than me.

My grandma and grandad, like a door without a key,
Always helping, having me round for tea.

Those are the things that matter to me.

Tom Harmer (11)
Holbrook High School, Ipswich

Imagination

What matters to me most is imagination
My imagination went wild once
There were swirls and pearls and little tiny curls
And bees with knees
And cell phones with cheese

My imagination went wild once
There were little licking lotuses
And a house with a mouth
There were different coloured moons
Some happy, some sad

My imagination went wild once
There was rugby with a twist
And food with a kick
And life drawn into a picture

My imagination went wild once
And it hasn't happened since
There was blue grass and green sky

My imagination went wild once
And I absolutely loved it!

Emerson Lee-Scott (11)
Holbrook High School, Ipswich

What Matters To Me

What matters to me . . .

Lots of things matter to me,
Though I cannot list them all,
But inside my head I'll let you see,
A selection rather small.

All the seasons are really nice,
I enjoy them all,
The way the sun melts the ice,
The way the leaves drift in the fall.

I enjoy all kinds of music
And I play the guitar,
I like to play things really quick,
Or emphasise each bar.

I'm a fussy eater too,
My favourite food is pizza,
The things I like are rather few,
If it's not margherita.

My friends are great and really cool,
I don't know where I'd be without them,
At the woods I play with them all,
And we make a really good den.

Last but not least, my family,
They matter most of all,
These are the things that matter to me,
In my list that is quite small.

Alfie Vaughan (11)
Holbrook High School, Ipswich

What Matters To Me?

It matters to me because it matters to me,
My fun, frantic family means a lot to me.

Warm, snug and cosy homes are the best,
It matters to me because it matters to me.

Big blue bear hidden in my bed is the best of all,
Books scattered by the side of my bed.

It matters to me because it matters to me,
My cool cats, chilled chickens, delightful dogs.

Big ones, small ones, over the shoulder ones,
All of these bags matter to me.

It matters to me because it matters to me.

Aoife Treacy (11)
Holbrook High School, Ipswich

What Matters To Me

Ask me something I'd forget,
Passer-by I never met,
Being happy is what matters to me,
My love, my friends, my family.

I have a cat, his name is Sox!
He came to me in a cardboard box.
He is lovely and funny and has a white chest,
He has white paws and a furry vest . . .

And that's what matters to me!

Sarah Roberts (11)
Holbrook High School, Ipswich

What Matters To Me Is Something Different

It's not
A rolling acrobat

It's not
The blazing sun

It's not
A gnome in the garden or the chippy down the road

It's not
The latest movie

It's not
The latest film, but I can tell you this

It's not
As small as a bug, not as big as the web

It's not
As small as a blade of grass or big as a tree

No . . .

It's this poem, this poem as wonderful as can be
This poem, this poem goes down in history!

Kyle Hammersley (11)
Holbrook High School, Ipswich

What Matters To Me The Most!

What matters to me the most is:
My family of course
They comforted me through their divorce
But now they're together
And we'll be happy forever
It's my family of course!

What matters to me the most is:
My hamster called Vampster
Vicious but cute
And surely not minute
She died this morning
And I'm still mourning
It's my hamster called Vampster to me!

What matters to me most
Is spending time at the coast
With the yucky sand sandwiches
And the yummy ice creams
I love spending time at the coast
That's me!

Dani Mills (11)
Holbrook High School, Ipswich

The Noise Creators

Bang, bang, bang! Go the drums next door,
Clap, clap, crash! They go thumping down the stairs.
The wall starts to dampen as they turn on the shower,
Hearing this, my poor old granny starts to cower.
I try to ignore the racket, sitting at the desk,
But how can you ignore it when you're doing your prep?
Wail, wail, wail, their baby's joined in too,
I hear a great thud as someone throws a shoe.
Papa closes his eyes, sighing in his grief,
Everybody sits silently, waiting for them to stop.
The wall suddenly collapses and lands with a boom,
Now, we are going to share the same big room.
They are, after all, my neighbours,
They are uncivil, annoying pests
That can't live in peace and quiet,
Although I wish they would.

Helen Sychta (12)
Ibstock Place School, London

Starry, Starry Night

Vincent's eyes saw light in shadow,
His hands painted colour when there was none,
His mind expanded to make the world brighter,
Exchanging the moon for the solitary sun.

The clouds were a torrent on stormy seas,
The flames a red rose pricking his mind,
People in the village peacefully sleeping,
Unaware of the part they played in his life.

Silhouettes in never-ending night-time,
Threatening Vincent's sanity,
Temporarily colour sets him free,
Who are we not to understand him?

Rhiannon Griffiths (13)
King Arthur's Community School, Wincanton

The House

House, home
House is safe for you
House is everything
House is like mother
House looks like a big box
My house, my room
House seating and watching TV
House smells like cup of chocolate
House, head of home and family
House, happy family.

Asie Jakubowa (13)
King Arthur's Community School, Wincanton

A Home Full Of Freedom

Secrets behind closed doors,
The place where comfort is found.
The freedom of emotion
And the laughter that lies beyond;
That's what I call home.

The family history is stored away,
Safe and snug from intruders.
The love and security,
The warmth and the hugs;
That's what I call home.

The protection and the security;
I love the place where I feel safe,
That's what I call home.

The love that's trapped within a building,
That's what I call home.

Hollie Biss (12)
King Arthur's Community School, Wincanton

The House

The house that's warm,
The house that's safe,
The house that is better
Than any other place

The house with your family,
The house that is clean,
The house with more love
Than any place that you've seen

The house with tables,
The house with the chairs,
The house with the worktops
And the house with the stairs

The house with the shower,
The house with the sink,
The house with the bedrooms
And Dad's half full drink

The house where you're happy,
The house where you're sad,
The house you're confined to
If you are bad

The house with the helpfulness,
The house with the care,
The house with the abandoned
Ragged teddy bear

The house with the boys,
The house with the girls,
The house with the old doll
With long, golden curls

The house where you're welcome,
The best place you've known,
This house isn't any house,
This house is a home.

Catherine Parker (14)
King Arthur's Community School, Wincanton

Finally Home

The family scent when you walk through the door,
The homely comforts greet you at your welcome,
With the safe feeling when you're inside,
And the click of the key,
When the door locks.

Inside the warmth hits you like a bomb,
The feeling of freedom flows through you,
And the scenes around paint themselves in your mind.

The smell of your mother's cooking in the kitchen,
With the radio playing sweet music,
The crackle of the fire,
And the slight glow of the flames,
Burn until they die.

Home is a place of love,
And you miss that love when you're away,
Homesick is a poison,
That makes you feel sad.

That's the place where you want to be,
When you're upset and need care,
You don't need to pretend now,
Home is always there . . .

Holly Turk (13)
King Arthur's Community School, Wincanton

My Home

What makes a house a home?
Photos of memories lining the walls,
Ornaments collected over the years,
Many years,
All of our things,
Special,
The place where Mum cooks the tea,
The place where I laugh and cry,
A place where we make mistakes,
But it's all right,
The place where we sleep,
Where we rest,
A place where friends come over,
And we gossip and laugh,
A place with a friendly atmosphere,
A place where you could walk in, in tears,
And its warmth embraces you in its arms,
It's all right,
Where problems can be caused,
And solved,
A place where you can be yourself,
Where you can dance in your room with your music up loud,
Sing and have fun,
A place you can call home.

Samantha Hurlow (13)
King Arthur's Community School, Wincanton

My Home Poem

I lay down with my head buried in the pillow
With the warmth of the roaring fire
I can hear Mum and Dad talking casually on the sofa
With the buzz of the news in the background
My cat leaps up on the sofa and purrs to her heart's content
Lying elegantly on my stomach
The smell of luxurious apple crumble lingers in the air
I can see the flame of a candle rippling like a wild river
I can see the shiny moon and the shimmering stars in the dark sky
The warmth of the fire brings me to a peaceful sleep
With stars watching me up above I feel safe
Home sweet home.

Lauren Armson (12)
King Arthur's Community School, Wincanton

Poem About My House

The puppy running around the garden,
Young kids falling around with bundles of energy,
Mum and Dad sprinting everywhere trying to keep the children quiet,
All sitting round the dinner table exhausted.

The old dog now plodding slowly around the garden.
Moving onto secondary school with so much fear,
Going over to the skate park with my best mates,
Being invited for sleepovers every other night.

Walking past the old dog's grave every morning.
Getting that first proper girlfriend.
Going to take that terrifying driving test.
Packing all those bags ready for that long trip to university.

Frank Higgins (11)
King Arthur's Community School, Wincanton

Home Sweet Home

I was there.
I saw it all.

But not everyone survived.
Going through the valley of death.

I sent a postcard from the house.
'I'm coming home, just keep waiting.'

Going through the fields,
Seeing the Chinook going over our head.

Lowering.
Lowering.
Lowering.

It was lowered until it came to the ground.
Going home.

The yellow taxi.
At my house.

The doorbell rang.
The door opened.

The world is in slow motion.
The tears from my mother.

I'm not sure if it was sad tears
Or happy tears.

Home sweet home!

George Heal (12)
King Arthur's Community School, Wincanton

A Winter's Day Has Come

A nother winter's day has come,

W illiam has left,
 I n the cold,
N ever happy,
T hat is William.
E mily, his mum, still crying,
R ichard, his dad, comforting her.
S adness is lingering.

D reaming memorable dreams is Will,
A nd now he dreams,
Y es, he dreams,

H ome . . .
A nother winter's day has come,
S adness is lingering.

C ome home, come home, his parents say.
O ptions are open, he can come home.
M aybe, just maybe, he will come home.
E verything turns for the better - Will is home.

Matthew Callard-Weller (12)
King Arthur's Community School, Wincanton

The Door Will Be Open, Always

A warm place on a rainy day,
A place of laughter, a place to play.
A place to be happy, a place to have fun,
Where the spreading of love first began.

Even on the dullest days,
The door will be open, always.
It will always be a place where you can go,
It will always be, forever so.

A roaring fire to warm you up,
Some steaming tea, in a cup.
A drawing or painting on a wall,
Never unwelcoming, never at all.

Even on the dullest days,
The door will be open, always.
It will always be a place where you can go,
It will always be, forever so.

A place of safety, security too,
A cosy place for me and you.
The appetising smell of cooking tea,
Served with love, especially for me.

Even on the dullest days,
The door will be open, always.
It will always be a place where you can go,
It will always be, forever so.

But as you're warm in your house,
Spare a moment for everybody else.
Perhaps those without homely pleasures,
Those without family treasures.

While you're cosy in your bed,
What will be going through your head?
Some don't even have a place to sleep,
But I don't hear them complain or weep!

So . . .
Although your home may be great,
Think of others beyond your mate.

Make the most of what you have
And treat it with great care,
Because some don't have a lovely home
Or a warm place to share.

Even on the dullest days,
The door will be open, always.
It will always be a place where you can go,
It will always be, forever so.

Abi Butt (12)
King Arthur's Community School, Wincanton

Living On The Streets!

Cold and lonely, sad and hurt,
Nobody to care for him, nobody to love him,
Crying with hunger, praying for warmth,
As he gives a little yawn.
He falls asleep on his ripped sheets
As the cardboard shelters him from the rain and sleet
That covers his feet on the cold concrete.
People walking past,
Some don't care, some just stare,
Some understand as he holds out his begging hands.
What will he do, where will he go?
He sits all alone and just doesn't know.
Hoping and wishing that maybe some day at last,
This life of despair will be a thing of the past.

Clare Ashford (11)
King Arthur's Community School, Wincanton

Who Matters To Me?

When I think about what matters to me, it seems to pass my eye,
The people in front of me, on whom I can rely.
I could have chosen to write about racism, world peace etc
But what about those who are so very important to me?

Forget material items, although they are a pleasure
What about those who I will forever and always treasure?
Some have known me for a little while, some all my life
And I know that I could go to them when in trouble or in strife.

Cliché as it sounds, I love every single one
And the amount they have done for me is second to none.
So next time I am asked what matters to me, instead of looking far and wide
I'll turn to those who have and will always be right by my side.

Georgina Ramsay (12)
King Edward VI Handsworth School, Birmingham

92

Green Pigs

What matters to me is the hatred for green,
The colour green is so unclean and obscene.
I'd like a colour that is fresh and pristine,
Not boring and common like the sad colour green.
What matters to me is pigs,
How dirty and odd, like the smell of a cod fish
And how they laze all day while they graze from the ground
And make that horrible, snorting, groggy sound,
While wallowing around in their own dirty filth
And tossing their heads towards the mud-ridden hills.
I dunno.
All I know is that if I saw a green pig, it would really annoy me
And wouldn't it be a sight to see?

Amy Grierson (12)
Middlewich High School, Middlewich

What Matters To Me!

I might look quiet, calm and mild,
But underneath I'm a wild child!
I hang off bars and jump out of trees,
Then I cut and bruise both of my knees.
It matters to me that my imagination is crazy,
I'm healthy, fit, definitely not lazy.
All of my dreams are strange and bonkers,
People think my head's been hit with a million conkers!
It matters to me that my life is fun,
Playing out and relaxing in the sun!

Katie Connell (11)
Middlewich High School, Middlewich

I Love To Dance

I love to dance,
In dance we prance,
I dance with Kate,
Cos she's my mate.
In rock 'n' roll dancing
We do most prancing,
Next is freestyle,
That is my style.
Street's exciting but
Very uninviting.
So I love to dance,
But I would rather be in a trance,
When it comes to break dance,
Flexibility is my strongest difficulty,
When we get lifted we need to trust,
Otherwise our dance could go bust!
Dance is great because
I get to dance with my best mate!

Mya Cross (12)
Middlewich High School, Middlewich

Make-Up Madness!

I love my make-up, it shows who I am,
I wear it on the weekend, as much as I can.
The lip gloss, the eyeliner, I have it all,
And when I want some more, I just go to the mall!
If I ever lost my make-up, I'd be distraught,
So if anyone tried to steal it they would be caught!
I wish I could wear it all day, oh I really do,
But if I wore it at school, the teachers would tell me to wipe it off in the loo.

Megan Berey (11)
Middlewich High School, Middlewich

94

What Matters To Me

Ice cream,
Smiley faces,
Tangerine.

I hate all braces,
However, I like strawberry laces.
Braces make my voice funny,
So the weather is never ever bright and sunny.
They make my teeth gorgeously straight
But they really do irritate.
In my mouth they feel like a metal gate,
But for the amount of time I have to wait,
I'd rather them give me braces on another date,
Just like my good old best mate.

Katie Lightfoot (11)
Middlewich High School, Middlewich

Books, Books

Books are the centre of my universe
My choice for books is diverse
Big or small, I'll read ten
Unlike others who can't be bothered with them
I'll read books to the end of dawn
Then at school all I can do is yawn.

Morgan Harrison (11)
Middlewich High School, Middlewich

What Matters To Me!

What matters to me is football.

They start to come out onto the pitch,
As the managers start to snitch,
The striker hits a thunder bolt,
As the other players stand at a halt.
The goalkeeper starts to tremble,
While the opposition hit the ball to Kendal.
The players shout to him, 'Watch out!'
As a supporter starts to clout.
Football is a game of teamwork,
While other sportsmen start to smirk.

Natasha Harrop (11)
Middlewich High School, Middlewich

What Matters To Me?

What matters to me . . .

M y family matter to me!
Y ou matter to me!

L ife matters to me.
I f I was a famous person it would matter to me.
F riends matter to me.
E arth matters to me.

A lot of things matter to me
And what I get I should take care of!

Kyran Gibson (12)
Middlewich High School, Middlewich

What Matters To Me

What matters to me are horses
How they gallop their way round the show jumping courses

When I sit in my saddle with my horse galloping all the way
I can't help but shout yay!

My beautiful pony is sometimes lonely
When his best friend, Harley, comes in to eat his barley

When I go to catch my pony he runs away to eat his hay
But I shout, 'Please stay!'

Chloe Scott (12)
Middlewich High School, Middlewich

Ode To Echo

So lithe and lovely, as she came,
Calling her patient lover's name,
Across the bower in autumn's mist,
Her lips were parted, sunlight kiss'd,
She walked through shade and over stream,
Her eyes half open, in a dream.

Inside the cave was damp and cold,
Her voice at first quiet then bold,
Call'd out her name as if a prayer,
To hear it whisper'd - someone there?
She call'd again - he'd know her voice,
He, her beloved, golden choice.

He'd spring from darkness, with sweetest charms,
And words of love, she in his arms,
But no, the darkness did resound,
To bounce her name back, hollow sound,
And so she cried, her voice afraid,
To hear the same from blackness shade.

She then sank down on knees bare,
No more to bathe in sunlight's glare,
She lay upon the gloomy ground,
And shrank until remain'd a sound,
O excellent, for thy love to pine,
I wish my love as great as thine.

Liam Hill (16)
Newton Abbot College, Newton Abbot

What Matters To Me

What I do five days a week
Each for an hour or more
Swimming is a talent I shall keep
I will love it for evermore.

My inspiration is Rebecca Adlington
And the diver, Tom Daley, too
You may call them my hero or heroine
The way they train is outstanding and committed too.

In PE at school
I end up not swimming at all
Instead, to my classmates' delight
I teach them backstroke and front crawl!

I owe a lot to my coach, Lisa
Who pushes me to the best of my ability
And when I get a personal best
I know there is always a hug waiting for me!

I am a part of Newton Abbot swimming team
Me, my mates and all of our club
We have a team spirit
We always scream and cheer (especially when we've won!).

27 medals I own
I am proud of every one
I know when I'm racing I'm not alone
Everybody hoping and cheering me on.

I hope to get more great times
I wish to watch myself on TV
I love swimming, I will swim all my life
Swimming is what matters to me!

Rachel Spooner (12)
Newton Abbot College, Newton Abbot

Mango's Story - A Tale Of Neglect

I was once the colour of
Melting marmalade;
I once breathed fire through
Flared nostrils
As my gallop pounded the paddock
My chocolate mane flung
The sun's rays back
Into welcome blue skies
And wispy clouds;
My glorious tail whipped
The air about me.
My heart was strong,
My life was
Full. In the
Leap and canter
Of confident youth.
I thought nothing could go wrong.

No familiar squelch of boots in the mud
Outside my stable door.
No voice warm as
Milk;
No hands
Which opened with sugared treats.
At twilight,
As I hear the scraping shut of my stable door,
I wonder
If the morning will bring the familiar warm voices,
Curry combs and bustling hands
Carrying buckets.
As the moon rises
And the shadows lurch in the darkness,
I scrape my hoof
Against the stable floor
To remind me that life is
Precious
And that once it was a
Pendulum
In the balance

As my time
Stood
Still.
Each evening I wonder whether the following day will again bring me
The chance to draw breath.

Catline Hill (14)
Newton Abbot College, Newton Abbot

The Day After 9/11

110 storeys fell on me today
I thought the hurt would never go away.
When I finally realised where I was at,
Well, it was at Heaven's door that I sat.
I sobbed and sobbed, even though it was over,
Gone,
Done and dusted some people might say.
People slumped around in discontent
But I rise and say,
'Even though people have died this day,
We stay free,
Even though two towers have fallen,
We stay free.'
So what if people like me are standing in dismay
At the pearly-white gates of Heaven this day?
What do we stay? We stay free!
And we will fight for our freedom
And as in God we trust,
He will show us the way, on this unforgettable day.

David Sparrow (13)
Oaklands Catholic School, Waterlooville

The Pain Of The Light

Night fading, dreams wavering,
Hope slipping through our fingertips,
As worry and regret are reborn;
And the serene emptiness of sleep is broken
By the orange-yellow, shapeless glow;
Shedding light on yet another endless day.

Hilla Hamidi (11)
Paddington Academy, London

102

To A Friend . . .

A friend that is one of a kind,
A friend that is perfect,
A friend who is hard to find.
A friend that is sweet,
A friend that you know will always be there.
A friend that is smart.
A friend that is loved by all.
A friend that never lets you fall.
A friend that you can talk to.
The whole world will know what a great person she is.
A friend I shall never forget.
She never lets me down.
Best of all the friends I've ever met.

Nural Ismail (11)
Paddington Academy, London

Delicious Fast Food

Delicious fast food,
Who cares for fish, chocolate cake
Or any other dish?

Delicious fast food,
Juicy and hot,
Even when it's in a pot.

Delicious fast food,
Fat or thin,
No one would want to throw it in the bin.

Delicious fast food,
Do you want it now?
I'm eating a burger made from a cow!

Mayharun Nessa (11)
Paddington Academy, London

The Mirror

When I look into the mirror,
I look very fine,
I think I look very pretty,
But my mum thinks I look divine,
Before I look into the mirror,
I change into my favourite top,
When the mirror sees me,
The mirror goes *pop!*

Tania Mufti (11)
Paddington Academy, London

Mother

What I feel for you is love,
You're an angel sent from above,
You're always in my heart,
You make the best lemon tarts,
It's you I adore,
I love you all the more,
Whatever is wrong of mine,
I just talk to you
And everything will be fine,
Mum, you're so kind,
Mum, you're so divine.

Arza Zenuni (11)
Paddington Academy, London

Who Am I?

Maybe, just maybe,
At the end of the road,
I will see a light,
It will guide me home,
It will lead me through the darkness,
And finally I'll see,
It's not about my image,
People love me for me.

Maybe, just maybe,
My perspective will change,
I will not feel ugly,
I will not feel ashamed.
And when this time comes,
I will feel a sense of self,
A sense of acceptance,
Of better mental health.

Now, now I know,
I know who I am,
I'm not alien to the world,
I'm like every other man.
I have found my conscience,
I have found my soul,
I have found my motivation,
To achieve my goals.

Jade Thomas (13)
Paddington Academy, London

Open A Book . . .

. . . Enter a freedom to listen, to run
Where will you look
Down in the earth or up to the sun?
Who will you meet
A thorn in the soul or an angel of light?
And what will you see?

What will it be?

Where will you go
A place full on heat or a place choked in snow?
And is it divine
Or somewhere that's lost in the heart of time?

What are the chances, what if its fate?
A vision in wood that you can't escape
Is it a dream or is it a hell?
What if it's both and your mind can't tell?
Who is the master? Who is the pawn?
What do you see when the shadows form?
Is it a horror or is it face
Laughing in time to your last mistake?
Seems like the rhythm is running amok
You're lost in your head and you've run out of luck

Why is it evil?
What do you fear?
Why is it cold
And dark in here?

How will you fare?
Will nobody care?

Oh, somebody look

It's only a book.

Timothy Manton [17]
Peter Symonds College, Winchester

Darkness

Swirling, blanketing, covering,
Ensnaring, blocking, eliminating.

The darkness is freed,
Half the cycle begins.

The other half has finished,
Another day complete.

What happens now?

Lewis Pilcher (15)
Richard Lander School, Truro

What Matters To Me

I love it when I score a goal in football,
I love it when I eat food,
I love it when I watch TV,
I love it when I go on my scooter,
I love it when I tackle people older than me.

I am a footballer,
I am a good eater,
I am a gamer,
I am a sports fan,
I am a runner,
I am a scorer.

I hate it when I don't get my way,
I hate it when I don't play football.

Danyal Ley-Seccombe (11)
Richard Lander School, Truro

The Jungle Man

I am a man who lives in the jungle.
I love it when I swing from vine to vine.
I hate it when people come to my island
And take my family to the zoo.
My family is the ape family.

Jonathan Wills (11)
Richard Lander School, Truro

What Matters To Me

I am a sailor.
I am a natural at it.
I am a great racer.
I am a good sportsman.

I hate it when there is no wind.
I hate it when I am not allowed to sail.
I hate it when I am beaten.
I hate it when I am told how to sail.

Kieran Smith (11)
Richard Lander School, Truro

I Am A . . .

I am a super duper dancer
I swivel in the wind
When the tempo gets faster
I start to move around
I can jump to the ceiling
And I do the splits to the ground
I wear fancy dresses
Tutus and tap shoes.

Alabama Seymour (11)
Richard Lander School, Truro

What Matters To Me

I am a game player
I am a footballer
I am a biker
I am a food eater
I am a sports fan
I am a football supporter

I love it when Matthew Troughton makes me laugh
I love it when Arsenal scores
I love it when I score in football
I love it when I eat food
I love it when I level up on Call of Duty Modern Warfare 2
I love it when I swim

I hate it when I get detention
I hate it when I miss an open goal
I hate it when I die on COD
I hate it when Arsenal lose.

Mathew Tapson (11)
Richard Lander School, Truro

The Emotions Of Me

I love it when I go to sleep listening to the sea
I love it when it's quiet and peaceful
I love it when all goes well
I love it when I succeed
I love it when I hear good news
I love it when I'm at peace with the world
Unfortunately life rarely turns out how you plan.

I hate it when it all goes wrong
I hate it when life doesn't go to plan
I hate it when it's a Monday morning
I hate it when the Coke has gone flat
I hate it when people are racist because it isn't right
I hate it when people are sexist because it also isn't right
Luckily life isn't too bad.

Nathan Hope (14)
Richard Lander School, Truro

What Matters To Me

I love it when my mum makes food
I love it when my dog wants me to stroke her
I love it when my friend says I can dance
I love it when Mathew Tapson makes me laugh

I hate it when my brothers beat me up
I hate it when my cat bites me while I stroke her
I hate it when my mum tells me off
I hate it when I get detention.

Matthew Troughton (11)
Richard Lander School, Truro

What Matters To Me

I am a champion sparrer
I am a gamer
I am a footballer
I am a movie watcher
I am a scooter rider
I am a walker
I am a body boarder
I am a climber

I love it when I go down a half pipe
I love it when I win a sparring match
I love it when I score a goal
I love it when I am on my Xbox 360
I love it when I eat.

Zak Hubbard (11)
Richard Lander School, Truro

I Am A Cat Lover

I am a cat lover.
I love them when they go and sit on your lap.
They are really sweet so they come and cuddle in.

I love it when they just look at you for a while.
I love it when they hide in the weirdest places.
I love it so much when they see food and run.

I hate it when it is night and their miaows wake us up.
I hate it when they scream for food.
I hate it when they kill other animals.

Hannah Whitworth (11)
Richard Lander School, Truro

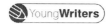

My Feelings Are . . .

I love it . . .
I love it when my family cooks me tea,
I love it when I get new friends and family,
I love it when I receive a funny joke,
I love it when I give my sister a poke,
I love it when I'm not ill,
I love it when I hear an opening till.

I am a . . .
I am a kitten sleeping peacefully in my bed,
I am a tiger resting my head,
I am a bee buzzing away,
I am a horse eating my hay,
I am a dog that gets hungry,
I am a cat that gets angry.

I hate it . . .
I hate it when an animal dies,
I hate it when a person lies,
I hate it when a car breaks down,
I hate it when my brother gives me a frown.

Jade Varley (12)
Richard Lander School, Truro

Poetry

I love it when I score a goal
I love it when I get a hug off my mum
I love it when I do my scootering
I love it when I do football
I love it when I get to do my running
I love it when I play rugby.

Luke Waters (11)
Richard Lander School, Truro

Love Days

I want to see you,
I want you back,
I need you now,
But I don't know where you are.

But I loved it when you sat next to me,
I loved it when you hugged me,
But I want you back.
I can't bear to be without you,
I love you so much,
So please come back,
I need you, I need you,
So come back.

I hated it when you left,
I hated when you did not call,
But I wish you'd come back,
Oh, just come back, oh just come back,
Because I love you, baby,
I love you.

Charlie Merrifield (11)
Richard Lander School, Truro

My Bed

What matters to me?
My bed.
I like my bed as it's where I rest my head.
On weekends I like to stay in bed for hours on end,
At the end of each day I go to bed ready for tomorrow.
I spend most of my time under the nice warm duvet.
My bed is small, so I curl up in a ball.
My bed has a duvet, two pillows and a mattress.
My bed is one of my favourite places to be in the world.
These are the reasons why I love my bed.

Ben Kent (13)
Richard Lander School, Truro

What Matters To Me

What matters to me
Is the sweet sound of music
You have loud, you have soft
It makes your mind go like bosh
But the best thing about it is
When you're depressed
All you gotta do is plug in some headphones
Or turn up the radio
To make your song come out from the rest
You have hip hop, you have screamo
You have beatbox and emo
You have classical
You have rap
But all that might be scrap
It's up to you what you like
Don't let anyone bring you down, alright?
Whether you're hidden away
Or out and about
Turn up your volume until they shout
It's what you like and what you want
Don't let anyone say what you can and can't like
Don't let them hit you like a bump
When you have one of those days
Just plug yourself away from the world
Just lay on your bed, curled
You're probably thinking what the hell is she on about?
But take my words in and hear me out.

Chloe Ellul (13)
Richard Lander School, Truro

114

What Matters To Me

What matters to me
I hear you guess
It might be my great aunt Bess
It could be my brother
Or my mother
Or the man of the house
We are strong
Maybe not single handedly
But together we are family
They matter to me
Every day they, I see
The love being shared
And the people that matter most
I mean this from the ghost
They give it all their soul
The love that makes us whole
Because we are family.

Mason Ireland (13)
Richard Lander School, Truro

Food

Food brings me pleasure,
But it affects the measure
Of the width of my tummy.
But all I say is,
'Mmm, that was yummy!'

Oscar Mackenzie (13)
Richard Lander School, Truro

What Matters To Me

What matters to me is my family and friends
They make me feel great and never debate.
We care and love and have the occasional row,
This year's gone well because of less ups and downs.
There have been no mistakes and no earthquakes,
We all should cheer and crack open the beer.
This year's going immense and I haven't felt tense.
My parents are great and have so much fun,
Even just sitting in the sun.
My brothers are bright and we always fight.
When there are arguments I sit in my room
Because all I can hear is a *boom, boom, boom.*
My brother's always sobbing because he never helps with the shopping,
It makes me mad when he is sad.
What matters to me is my family and friends.

Ben Keane (13)
Richard Lander School, Truro

Untitled

I love it when I get hot chocolate on a winter's night
For then it warms me up.
I love it when I go to the skate park
And go down all the ramps.
I love it when I get cake, especially sponge cake.
I love it when I get smoothies, including ones I make.

Paris Scott (12)
Richard Lander School, Truro

What Matters To Me

What matters to me
Are my pets and my family
My dad, my mother,
My dog and my half brother
My dog is a Jack Russell called Fred
He may be brainless but I'd care if he were dead
It is coming up for my brother's birthday
So I hope he has a nice one anyway
I didn't know what to get for him,
But I've got him his present now.
I'm sure that he'll enjoy it,
But he isn't old enough to say wow!

What matters to me are my friends
I really don't think that our friendship will end
Even though Thom drives me round the bend
Still he's my friend.
Me and Alex are best friends,
We have fallen out many times,
But our friendship never ends.

Alex Fryett (13)
Richard Lander School, Truro

What Matters To You?

What matters to me is my friends,
Always there for me, watching over me,
My friends, I would be nothing without them,
The ones I can trust and tell everything,
And still know they will never tell a soul.

Harry Lawrence (12)
Richard Lander School, Truro

What Matters To Me

These are my friends,
They're crazy and they're cool
And sometimes they act like fools.
They're brilliant and they are the best
And simply better than all the rest.

There is Alannah,
Who is the mad horsey lover,
There is Lissy,
Who is obsessed with Twilight
And the one and only Kayleigh,
Who likes to glam herself up.

We always have so much fun,
Dancing and playing around in the sun,
Because we always stick together
And spend time together.
These are the girls that will last forever.
Best friends.

Shannon Gray (14)
Richard Lander School, Truro

Friends

What matters to me are my friends,
Friends are my life and my passion,
Friends are people who will stick with you through the hard times,
Friends are people who will support you no matter what,
Friends are people who will help you get better and cheer you up
When you are feeling down,
Friends will trust you and you can tell them anything.
What matters to me are my friends.

Sarah Bennett (13)
Richard Lander School, Truro

What Matters To Me

What matters to me,
Is my pet cat, Sam.
He sits there in the chair,
Cleaning and licking his hair.

What matters to me,
Is my family.
They are always there,
Even if I'm not here.

What matters to me,
Are my hobbies.
If I'm not on my motorbike,
I'll be fixing a leaky pipe.

What matters to me,
Is my friends.
I don't know what I'd do without them,
Even if they drive me round the bend.

Jed Hope (13)
Richard Lander School, Truro

I Love It When . . .

I love it when I go on my skateboard.
I love it when I go to the beach.
I love it when I roll down a hill.
I love it when I bake buns in the kitchen.

Daniel Roberson (11)
Richard Lander School, Truro

What Matters To Me

What matters to me is my family,
Spending time together,
The friendship lasts forever.
Going on holiday, having so much fun,
Playing in the sea and sitting in the sun.
Through all the ups and downs,
My sister always acts like a clown.

Happy faces, sad faces,
We are all in it together, no matter what.
All of the bad things are forgot,
And all the good things are not.
They mean so much to me,
We are one big, happy family.
What matters to me is my family!

Alexandrea Hunter (13)
Richard Lander School, Truro

What Matters To Me - My Friends And Family

F riends are funny, happy and kind
R eally they are
I love my friends, they help me when I'm down. My friends are
E xcellent, marvellous, amazing and helpful, I would
N ever lose them
D on't be mean to them or I will be
S ad.

What matters to me is my family,
I love them and they love me.
They help me when I'm sad,
Or when I feel bad.
We always have fun in the sun,
I love my mum, she is the best,
She is better than all the rest.

Jodie MacQueen (13)
Richard Lander School, Truro

What Matters To Me

Domestic violence
Don't suffer in silence
Retain your life
Maybe get a new wife

Don't just pout
Go on, get out
Strike a pose
Don't turn up your nose

Suffer the measures
In the end you'll have pleasures

Domestic violence
Don't suffer in silence
Your life will be destroyed
But not by an asteroid

This will be your final chance
Go on do it
Because then you have dance
End domestic violence now!

Jennifer Lovering (13)
Richard Lander School, Truro

Chocolate

I eat chocolate
I eat sweets
I eat bonbons
I eat treats
I eat candy
I eat chews
I eat everything
Unless it's shoes!

Katie Platts (12)
Richard Lander School, Truro

What Matters To You?

My family is
What matters to me,
Their undying love
And guidance is free.

They care and support,
Through troubled times,
A shoulder to cry on
And a voice that's sublime.

With advice in abundance
And love in their heart,
Their wisdom helps guide me
To live life from the start.

The first stuttering words,
The first steps I sway,
Are learnt from my family
Who I will owe to this day.

They taught me politeness,
Manners and respect,
To kick start my adulthood
And make it perfect.

They taught me courteousness
And made me able to see,
That they know best
When to set me free.

My family is
What matters to me,
Their support, selflessness
And compassion is key.

Harry Searle (13)
Richard Lander School, Truro

What Matters To You?

R unning
U nion
G oal kicking
B all
Y outh academy

F oul
O ffside
O pposition
T ackling
B all
A ttacker
L eft back
L eft wing

X box Live
B eneficial buy
O utstanding
X box market place

S ettled
L ovely
E njoyable
E ssential
P eaceful
I deal
N ecessary
G enuine dream

F un
A ssociation
C ommunication
E ducational
B rilliant
O rderly
O riginal
K nowledge.

Adam Britland (13)
Richard Lander School, Truro

All Of This Is Cornwall To Me

A rushing river
A bubbling creek
A silent stream
All of these are Cornwall to me

Pounding waves
Rolling breakers
Spitting tubes
All of these are Cornwall to me

Big waves
Small waves
Fun waves
All of these are Cornwall to me

A running fox
A startled rabbit
A chirping cricket
All of these are Cornwall to me

A place of fun, of joy, of friendship
A place of surf, of waves, of beaches
A place of sun, of sky, of water
All of these are Cornwall to me

A place of home
This is Cornwall to me.

Louis Mavor (15)
Richard Lander School, Truro

Snow

Gently to the ground falls the snow
Ever so soft and very slow
In the evening or at midday
Falling onto children at play
Also landing on white trees
Snowflakes fall wherever they please
One by one the casements catch
The silvery-white roof made of thatch
Crouched in white kennel, like a log
With pearly-white paws sleeps the dog
Round the garden the robins hop
And all around the white-roofed shop
A stream that has turned into ice
Looks all sparkly and very nice
Scampering squirrels gather nuts
And keep them safe from nasty mutts
Curled up in a snuggly ball
The dormouse won't wake up till fall
Cold as ever still, the snow
Just carries on her gentle flow.

Natasha Brookes (15)
Richard Lander School, Truro

The Old Man

An old man wanders through the wild winter weather,
His head and his heartstrings no longer sewn together.
He fumbles through the darkness with a beast at his side,
His long cloak billowing like the rolling tide.
A thousand years of pain apparent in his face,
His mind shut away in a faraway place.
His boots worn from walking and his stomach devoid of food,
He blunders to the cliff face, knowing life is little good.
His one remaining friend whimpers into the night,
Wanting his master to stay in his sight.
He smiles for the last time as the sun cracks through the sky,
He leaves the world forever, bidding it goodbye.
And on nights when the wind goes on a deathly mission,
And your mind jumps to thoughts of spirits and superstition,
And you're beside a wild sea and a chill goes through your spine,
You may see an old man walking, with tears frozen in his eyes.

Bethany Howell (15)
Richard Lander School, Truro

Gull

I perch on a lamp post,
Staring down at the show's host,
I fly out to sea,
My heart filled with glee.
Suddenly, I drop off on a tourist,
As I fly by a great fat walrus.

Over there is a man with a pasty,
If I steal it, he may get nasty.
Oh well, I'll take it anyway,
After all, he did take a shot at me.

Jago Penrose (14)
Richard Lander School, Truro

What Matters To Me

What matters to me
Is my family
They mean so much
We love, we care and such
I have had a rough time this year
As my dad has been drinking down the beer
He has been sneaking around like a mouse
Hiding his alcohol all over the house
My mum and dad were always shouting
But this time did not get over the mountain
Eventually me and my mum moved out
Leaving my dad and his doubt
My brother stayed with my dad
But leaving them behind I just felt so bad
I got so depressed
I thought to myself, I need a rest
I go to see my dad and brother
But I don't get to see much of the other
And just as I think things are getting better
I was in school and I got a letter
This letter was not good, it was bad and it said
My mum was in hospital, I was so sad
My mum still isn't well
And till this very day I feel like I'm in hell.

Fraser Hill (13)
Richard Lander School, Truro

What Matters To Me?

What matters to me?
War is poor
Terrorists don't knock at the door
They fight until there is no daylight
Strong men are put in fright
Men die
Men die because they try
What matters to me?
They sign up for the job
They could get shot by a terrorist
Men die
Why?
Why is asked?
That won't be answered
That I still ask
Guns go boom
Men will see doom
I hope my question is answered one day
Men die
The family cry
And I say goodbye.

Reece Light (13)
Richard Lander School, Truro

Portugal

Portugal is like a summer wonderland for me,
Sitting in the hot sun whilst eating a freshly barbecued sardine.
Surfing your heart out and snorkling for hours upon end,
The crystal clear waters sparkle, glitter and . . .

Elijah Francis (13)
Richard Lander School, Truro

Family

This is the one thing that matters to me,
My one and only family.
They are with me 24/7,
They will be by my side when I am in Heaven.

It matters to me where my family are,
Their eyes are like shiny stars.
From my heart filled with love,
They will notice from above

That I am not some mean little girl,
But a girl who thinks her family is her world.

They help me through bad and good,
They are as friendly and tasty as food.

They know when I am sad or alone,
They lead me up the path,
To my comforting and warm home.

There is one thing that matters to me,
That is my amazing family.

Erin Lynn (13)
Richard Lander School, Truro

Wintry Feeling

I love it when the air smells wintry.
I love it when I see my best friends laugh like hyenas.
I love it when the snow falls like a white blanket.
I love it when I see smiling faces.
I love it when my cat is stretching in front of the fire.
I love it when I see ancient paintings.

Kerenza Cattell (12)
Richard Lander School, Truro

What Matters To Me

What matters to me?
I know what matters to me!
Rugby matters.

Matt Banahan running down the wing
Schalk Burger too busy eye gouging
Nick Abendanon playing the game
Lewis Moody feels no pain.

Props: the big, fat boys
Locks is where you hear the noise
The back row shouting all the calls
Scrum half running in and out of walls.

Fly half doing all the kicks
Centres and wings following the chips.

Full back is just there all alone,
Mopping up all the mess and kicks
That go to him with a big, loud groan.

So, you know that I play the game
And you and I know my aim
So let me go away
To practise for my game
As I have rugby to play.

Jacob Englefield (13)
Richard Lander School, Truro

What Matters To You?

F oul
O ver-dramatic dives
O ppostion
T op notch players
B all flying into the goal
A ttitude
L eft wings
L egs breaking

C omputer games
O utstanding
M icrosoft Word
P rogrammes
U seful
T ranslator
E rror
R eceive emails

S ilent
L ie in
E asily fall asleep
E njoy
P leasant

B ed to sleep on
E njoyable peace
D esignated space
R eady to have time to yourself
O vertime slept
O pen space
M ess everywhere.

Aaron Crowhurst [12]
Richard Lander School, Truro

What Matters To Me?

What matters to me?
Books are the ones that matter.
They hold inside their binding, my world,
My glee.

If everyone hated me,
And all my family were dead,
I would still have my books,
My sanity.

Inside a book,
There is a land,
Forgotten by people afar,
Just look.

Whoever's reading this,
Maybe from a book,
Are now inspired to read
And feel my bliss.

Books matter to me,
Hard or soft.
The cover means nothing.
The pages hide the real secrecy.

Jimi Harrold (12)
Richard Lander School, Truro

What Matters To Me?

What matters to me,
Is my family and friends,
When we fall out we always make amends.
My mum and my dad
And my brother, Brad,
Who annoys me lots and makes me mad.
All matter to me.

What matters to me,
Is all my pets.
I spend a lot of time with them even if it's wet.
My cats sit on my mat
And my guinea pigs are very fat.
They all matter to me.

Leanna Rees (12)
Richard Lander School, Truro

Winter To Warm

I love it when it snows,
I love it when it is windy,
I love it when there is no school,
I love it when a fire is burning as bright as the sun,
I love it when it is warm,
I love it when I see a jet.

Jonathan Brown (12)
Richard Lander School, Truro

What Matters To You?

W hat matters to me?
H elping friends in distress.
A cting myself,
T aking life well.

M emories of the good times,
A nd of the bad.
T elling my friends,
T hey smell really bad!
E very minute passing by,
R ecalling stories of my parents' time,
S inging out loud, unaware there's no sound.

T alking to the rabbit,
O ut in the shed, imagining what life would be if I were he.

M y life is amazing.
E verybody is changing.

Mollie Jewell (12)
Richard Lander School, Truro

Everything I Love

I love it when my gecko licks his eyes clean
I love it when the surf is perfect
I love it when the hot African wind blows through France
I love it when the sky is as blue as blue
I love it when the sun is so hot, the tarmac hurts your feet
I love it when the rain hits the ground for the first time after a drought.

Luther Wolf (13)
Richard Lander School, Truro

Featured Poets:
DEAD POETS
AKA Mark Grist & MC Mixy

Mark Grist and MC Mixy joined forces to become the 'Dead Poets' in 2008.

Since then Mark and Mixy have been challenging the preconceptions of poetry and hip hop across the country. As 'Dead Poets', they have performed in venues ranging from nightclubs to secondary schools; from festivals to formal dinners. They've appeared on Radio 6 Live with Steve Merchant, they've been on a national tour with Phrased and Confused and debuted their show at the 2010 Edinburgh Fringe, which was a huge success.

Both Mark and Mixy work on solo projects as well as working together as the 'Dead Poets'. Both have been Peterborough's Poet Laureate, with Mixy holding the title for 2010.

The 'Dead Poets' are available for workshops in your school as well as other events. Visit www.deadpoetry.co.uk for further information and to contact the guys!

Read on to pick up some fab writing tips!

Your
WORKSHOPS

In these Workshops We are going to look at Writing styles and examine some literary techniques that the 'Dead Poets' use. Grab a pen, and let's go!

Rhythm Workshop

Rhythm in writing is like the beat in music. Rhythm is when certain words are produced more forcefully than others, and may be held for longer duration. The repetition of a pattern is what produces a 'rhythmic effect'. The word rhythm comes from the Greek meaning of 'measured motion'.

Count the number of syllables in your name. Then count the number of syllables in the following line, which you write in your notepad: 'My horse, my horse, will not eat grass'.

Now, highlight the longer sounding syllables and then the shorter sounding syllables in a different colour.

Di dum, di dum, di dum, di dum is a good way of summing this up.

You should then try to write your own lines that match this rhythm. You have one minute to see how many you can write!

Examples include:
'My cheese smells bad because it's hot'
and
'I do not like to write in rhyme'.

For your poem, why don't you try to play with the rhythm? Use only longer beats or shorter beats? Create your own beat and write your lines to this?

Did you know ... ?

Did you know that paper was invented in China around 105AD by Ts'ai Lun. The first English paper mill didn't open until 1590 and was in Dartford.

Rhyme Workshop

Start off with the phrase 'I'd rather be silver than gold' in your notepad. and see if you can come up with lines that rhyme with it -

'I'd rather have hair than be bald'
'I'd rather be young than be old'
'I'd rather be hot than cold'
'I'd rather be bought than sold'

Also, pick one of these words and see how many rhymes you can find:

Rose

Wall

Warm

Danger

What kinds of rhymes did you come up with? Are there differences in rhymes? Do some words rhyme more cleanly than others? Which do you prefer and why?

Onomatopoeia Workshop

Divide a sheet of A4 paper into 8 squares.

You then have thirty seconds to draw/write what could make the following sounds:

Splash	Ping
Drip	Bang
Rip	Croak
Crack	Splash

Now try writing your own ideas of onomatopoeia. Why might a writer include onomatopoeia in their writing?

Lists Workshop

Game - you (and you can ask your friends or family too) to write as many reasons as possible for the following topics:

Annoying things about siblings

The worst pets ever

The most disgusting ingredients for a soup you can think of

Why not try writing a poem with the same first 2, 3 or 4 words?

I am ...

Or

I love it when ...

Eg:

I am a brother

I am a listener

I am a collector of secrets

I am a messer of bedrooms.

Repetition Workshop

Come up with a list of words/phrases, aim for at least 5. You now must include one of these words in your piece at least 6 times. You aren't allowed to place these words/phrases at the beginning of any of the lines.

Suggested words/phrases:

Why

Freedom

Laughing

That was the best day ever

I can't find the door

I'm in trouble again

The best

Workshop
POETRY 101

Below is a poem written especially for poetry matters, by MC Mixy.
Why not try and write some more poems of your own?

What is Matter?

© MC Mixy

What matters to me may not be the same things that matter to you
You may not agree with my opinion mentality or attitude
The order in which I line up my priorities to move
Choose to include my view and do what I do due to my mood
And state of mind
I make the time to place the lines on stacks of paper and binds
Concentrate on my artwork hard I can't just pass and scrape behind
Always keep close mates of mine that make things right
And even those who can't … just cos I love the way they can try
What matters to me is doing things the right way
It's tough this game of life we play what we think might stray from what
others might say
In this world of individuality we all wanna bring originality
Live life and drift through casually but the vicious reality is
Creativity is unique
Opinions will always differ but if you figure you know the truth, speak
So many things matter to me depending on how tragically deep you wanna
go
I know I need to defy gravity on this balance beam
As I laugh and breathe draft and read map the scene practise piece smash
the beat and graphic release
Visual and vocal it's a standard procedure
Have to believe and don't bite the hand when it feeds ya

If you wanna be a leader you need to stay out of the pen where the sheep are
The things that matter to me are
My art and my friends
That will stay from the start to the end
People will do things you find hard to amend
Expect the attacks and prepare you gotta be smart to defend
I put my whole heart in the blend the mass is halved yet again
I'm marked by my pen a big fish fighting sharks of men
In a small pond
Dodging harpoons and nets hooks and predators tryna dismember ya
I won't let them I won't get disheartened I can fend for myself
As long as I'm doing what's important
I'm my mind where I'm supported is a just cause to be supporting
In these appalling hard times I often find myself falling when
Only two aspects of my life keep me sane and allow me to stand tall again
Out of all of them two is a small number
It's a reminder I remind ya to hold necessity and let luxury fall under
Try to avoid letting depression seep through
Take the lesson we actually need a lot less than we think we do
So what matters to you?
They may be similar to things that matter to me
I'm actually lacking the need of things I feel would help me to succeed
Though I like to keep it simple, I wanna love, I wanna breed
I'm one of many individuals in this world where importance fluctuates and varies
Things that matter will come and go
But the ones that stay for long enough must be worth keeping close
If you're not sure now don't watch it you'll know when you need to know
Me, I think I know now … yet I feel and fear I don't.

Turn overleaf for a poem by Mark Grist and some fantastic hints and tips!

Workshop
POETRY 101

What Tie Should I Wear Today?

© Mark Grist

I wish I had a tie that was suave and silk and slick,
One with flair, that's debonair and would enchant with just one flick,
Yeah, I'd like that … a tie that's hypnotizing,
I'd be very restrained and avoid womanising,
But all the lady teachers would still say 'Mr Grist your tie's so charming!'
As I cruise into their classrooms with it striking and disarming.
At parents' evenings my tie's charm would suffice,
In getting mums to whisper as they leave 'Your English teacher seems nice!'

Or maybe an evil-looking tie - one that's the business,
Where students will go 'Watch out! Mr Grist is
on the prowl with that evil tie.'
The one that cornered Josh and then ripped out his eye.
Yeah no one ever whispers, no one ever sniggers,
Or my tie would rear up and you'd wet your knickers.
Maybe one girl just hasn't heard the warning,
Cos she overslept and turned up late to school that morning,
And so I'd catch her in my lesson yawning … oh dear.
I'd try to calm it down, but this tie's got bad ideas.
It'd size the girl up and then just as she fears,
Dive in like a serpent snapping at her ears.
There'd be a scream, some blood and lots and lots of tears,
And she wouldn't be able to yawn again for years.

Or maybe … a tie that everyone agrees is mighty fine
And people travel from miles around to gawp at the design
I'd like that … a tie that pushes the boundaries of tieware right up to the limit
It'd make emos wipe their tears away while chavs say 'It's wicked innit?'
and footy lads would stop me with 'I'd wear that if I ever won the cup.'
And I'd walk through Peterborough to slapped backs, high fives, thumbs up
While monosyllabic teenagers would just stand there going 'Yup.'

I don't know. I'd never be sure which of the three to try
As any decision between them would always end a tie.

Tips and Advice for PERFORMING Your Poem

So you've written your poem, now how about performing it.
Whether you read your poem for the first time in front of your class, school or strangers at an open mic event or poetry slam, these tips will help you make the best of your performance.

Breathe and try to relax.

Every poet that reads in front of people for the first time feels a bit nervous, when you're there you are in charge and nothing serious can go wrong.

People at poetry slams or readings are there to support the poets. They really are!

If you can learn your poem off by heart that is brilliant, however having a piece of paper or notebook with your work in is fine, though try not to hide behind these.

It's better to get some eye contact with the audience.
If you're nervous find a friendly face to focus on.

Try to read slowly and clearly and enjoy your time in the spotlight.

Don't rush up to the microphone, make sure it's at the right height for you and if you need it adjusted ask one of the team around you.

Before you start, stand up as straight as you can and get your body as comfortable as you can and remember to hold your head up.

The microphone can only amplify what what's spoken into it; if you're very loud you might end up deafening people and if you only whisper or stand too far away you won't be heard.

When you say something before your poem, whether that's hello or just the title of your poem, try and have a listen to how loud you sound. If you're too quiet move closer to the microphone, if you're too loud move back a bit.

Remember to breathe! Don't try to say your poem so quickly you can't find time to catch your breath.

And finally, **enjoy!**

Poetry FACTS

Here are a selection of fascinating poetry facts!

No word in the English language rhymes with 'MONTH'.

William Shakespeare was born on 23rd April 1564 and died on 23rd April 1616.

The haiku is one of the shortest forms of poetic writing.
Originating in Japan, a haiku poem is only seventeen syllables, typically broken down into three lines of five, seven and five syllables respectively.

The motto of the Globe Theatre was 'totus mundus agit histrionem' (the whole world is a playhouse).

The Children's Laureate award was an idea by Ted Hughes and Michael Morpurgo.

The 25th January each year is Burns' Night, an occasion in honour of Scotland's national poet Robert Burns.

Spike Milligan's 'On the Ning Nang Nong' was voted the UK's favourite comic poem in 1998.

Did you know *onomatopoeia* means the word you use sounds like the word you are describing – like the rain *pitter-patters* or the snow *crunches* under my foot.

'Go' is the shortest complete sentence in the English language.

Did you know rhymes were used in olden days to help people remember the news? Ring-o'-roses is about the Plague!

The Nursery Rhyme 'Old King Cole' is based on a real king and a real historical event. King Cole is supposed to have been an actual monarch of Britain who ruled around 200 A.D.

Edward Lear popularised the limerick with his poem 'The Owl and the Pussy-Cat'.

Lewis Carroll's poem 'The Jabberwocky' is written in nonsense style.

POEM – noun

1. a composition in verse, esp. one that is characterized by a highly developed artistic form and by the use of heightened language and rhythm to express an intensely imaginative interpretation of the subject.

Poetry TIPS

We have compiled some helpful tips for you budding poets...

In order to write poetry, read lots of poetry!

Keep a notebook with you at all times so you can write whenever (and wherever) inspiration strikes.

Every line of a poem should be important to the poem and interesting to read. A poem with only 3 great lines should be 3 lines long.

Use an online rhyming dictionary to improve your vocabulary.

Use free workshops and help sheets to learn new poetry styles.

Experiment with visual patterns - does your written poetry create a good pattern on the page?

Try to create pictures in the reader's mind - aim to fire the imagination.

Develop your voice. Become comfortable with how you write.

Listen to criticism, and try to learn from it, but don't live or die by it.

Say what you want to say, let the reader decide what it means.

Notice what makes other's poetry memorable. Capture it, mix it up and make it your own. (Don't copy other's work word for word!)

Go wild. Be funny. Be serious. Be whatever you want!

Grab hold of something you feel - anything you feel - and write it.

The more you write, the more you develop. Write poetry often.

Use your imagination, your own way of seeing.

Feel free to write a bad poem, it will develop your 'voice'.

Did you know ...?

'The Epic of Gilgamesh' was written thousands of years ago in Mesopotamia and is the oldest poem on record.

Wordsmith

The *premier* magazine
for creative young people

A platform for your imagination and creativity. Showcase your ideas and have your say. Welcome to a place where like-minded young people express their personalities and individuality knows no limits.

For further information visit *www.youngwriters.co.uk*.

A peek into Wordsmith world ...

Poetry and Short Stories

We feature both themed and non-themed work every issue. Previous themes have included; dreams and aspirations, superhero stories and ghostly tales.

Next Generation Author

This section devotes two whole pages to one of our readers' work. The perfect place to showcase a selection of your poems, stories or both!

Guest Author Features & Workshops

Interesting and informative tutorials on different styles of poetry and creative writing. Famous authors and illustrators share their advice with us on how to create gripping stories and magical picturebooks. Novelists like Michael Morpurgo and Celia Rees go under the spotlight to answer our questions.

The fun doesn't stop there ...

Every issue we tell you what events are coming up across the country. We keep you up to date with the latest film and book releases and we feature some yummy recipes to help feed the brain and get the creative juices flowing.

So with all this and more, Wordsmith is *the* magazine to be reading.

If you are too young for Wordsmith magazine or have a younger friend who enjoys creative writing, then check out Scribbler!. Scribbler! is for 7-11 year-olds and is jam-packed full of brilliant features, young writers' work, competitions and interviews too. For further information check out *www.youngwriters.co.uk* or ask an adult to call us on (01733) 890066.

To get an adult to subscribe to either magazine for you, ask them to visit the website or give us a call.

What Matters To You?

I'd rather have a cat than a dog,
I'd rather get lost in the woods than a bog,
I'd rather have family than friends,
I'd rather be clever than at my wits' ends,
I'd rather have friends than money,
I'd rather have treacle than honey,
I'd rather be tall than a titch,
I'd rather be funny than rich,
I'd rather be ill than dead,
I'd rather be alive and fed,
I'd rather have a pig than a cow,
I'd rather end this poem now.

Ellie Faux (12)
Richard Lander School, Truro

It's My Life, Only Mine

I love it when I'm with Mum.
I love it when I'm with friends, wherever it is.
I love it when I can't stop smiling because 'he' spoke to me.
I love it when it's a cold day and I can cuddle down with a hot chocolate.
I love it when it's Christmas morning and I look at all the other houses,
thinking how happy all the children are.
I love it on New Year's Eve, waiting and watching.

Rose Pipkin
Richard Lander School, Truro

What Matters To Me Is Love

What matters to me is love,
It comes from the sky above,
It's pink or red in a little love heart,
Or a massive one filled with art.

What matters to me is love,
It comes from within a dove,
It comes and goes,
As the wind blows,
But no one knows,
What matters to me is love.

I love my friends and family,
We fit together happily,
When I am alone,
They take me home,
What matters to me is love.

Love is important, love is fine,
It comes and goes all the time,
Love is Cupid, with his bow and arrow,
It can turn thick and narrow.

It has its good times, it has its bad,
Sometimes it can be oh so sad,
J'adore is love, everyone hears it.

Tamzin Knuckey (13)
Richard Lander School, Truro

146

The Midnight Beach

When the sky is pitch-black and the moon is white
And everything is quiet on a cold winter's night
Go to the beach to watch the sea shining bright
Gaze at the water as it glistens with light

The beach is so quiet, it's the best place to be
It is a place to sit and be at one with the sea
Nowhere on Earth will you quite feel so free
So let's walk down to the ocean, just you and me

I can listen for hours to the sound of the ocean
Hear as the waves roll back and forth in motion
Watch all the birds approach it with caution
Only at night the sea comes alive with emotion

The golden sand is just like a moving floor
As the tide goes down it reveals some more
All the footprints washed away from the day before
All that's left is a blank canvas for you to explore.

But as the dawn begins to break rises the burning sun
A warning sign to tell you that morning's begun
And the night fades away to let the day have its run
Just 12 hours to wait until darkness succumbs.

Megan Lee (15)
Richard Lander School, Truro

Love And Hate

I hate it when seagulls sneakily take your pasty.
I hate it when bad memories from the past come back to haunt me.
I hate it when nerves paralyse my body.
I hate it when my sister and I fall out over nothing.
I hate it when bullies think they can control their victims.
I hate it when people treat animals unfairly.

I love it when my cat sits purring upon my chest because she's happy.
I love it when my family and I gently walk upon a sandy beach.
I love it when my family and I sit in front of a roaring winter fire.
I love it when my cats cheerfully greet me when I get home from school.
I love it when the sun sets upon a tired world.
I love it when my sister and I swing carelessly from trees.

Rebecca Pearce (14)
Richard Lander School, Truro

Time With Me

I love it when deep, dark mists
Cover the morning skies.
I love it when frost crackles
Like a spitting fire under my feet.
I love it when the sun shines bright lights
On the sea surface.
I love it when excitement hits you
And you feel all warm inside.
I love it when you get off a plane
And the burning heat hits your face.
I love it when I turn over my pillow
And it's refreshing and cool.
I love my life.

Benjamin Smith (12)
Richard Lander School, Truro

Bumblebee

The humble bumblebee
Not quite all as they seem
With their sting and buzzing noise
They land upon the leaves.

The way their fur is striped with
The colours yellow and black,
Collecting pollen all day long
Then always returning back.

I've always imagined the queen bee to wear a little crown
But to be honest, I don't think it would be able to scale down
The hot summer sun is always best for bees
As it makes the pretty flowers bloom and flourish you see.

I would love to be a bumblebee
The way they fly and buzz
And not forgetting their colourful fur
Which really is a must.

Eden Pilcher (13)
Richard Lander School, Truro

Everything I Love

I love it when it's a cold, crispy morning,
I love it when the morning dew lies on the grass,
I love it when snow hasn't been stepped on.

I love it when summer arrives like a new flower,
I love it when the sky is as blue as it could be,
I love it when my guinea pig squeaks in the morning.

Lauren Wroe (12)
Richard Lander School, Truro

Love/Hate Relationships

I love it when . . .
I step from the rattling carriage and smile into his face.
I lie awake at night thinking of things to dream of.
I snuggle and cuddle into warm and waiting shoulders.
I stare at still images and they bring back my memories.
Dramatic symphonies heighten and drive shivers through my spine.
I send a wry smile to a stranger and get one in return.

I hate it when . . .
Beliefs and faiths are laughed at, mocked and ridiculed.
Women are undermined, forgotten and seen as weak.
I am ignored simply for being myself.
Helpless animals are abused due to harsh, bipedal monsters.
People judge and stereotype without ever knowing truth.
I cry and blame myself for the stupidity of others.

Amy Stephens (14)
Richard Lander School, Truro

My Feelings

I love it when I drive to the airport.
I love it when I jump into the sea and feel the coldness.
I love it when I smell that Christmas smell.
I love it when the plane lands on the runway.
I love it when I drive in the night.

I hate it when there is war in the world.
I hate it when I forget what I was going to say.
I hate it when I get homework.
I hate it when I am ill.
I hate it when someone cries.
I hate it when someone dies.

Molly Kirton (14)
Richard Lander School, Truro

Guilty Love

He snatched her heart
And ignited it with love
Into her eyes he looked
As the stars sparkled above

Hand in hand
She had no clue
Of his next three words
'I love you'

His lips touched hers
The moment was spared
The world stood still
At the moment they shared

She gave out a smile
She gave out a light
Never had he seen
Her shine so bright

He stood at her side
And whispered to her
'Without your love
My life is a blur'

She looked at him
With deep despair
Trying to tell him
Her love was not there

The fire in her heart
That he had built
Was burning out
With anger and guilt

But he was a dreamer
She was a lie
Their calm, caring hearts
Drowned in a cry.

Amber Tithecott (14)
Richard Lander School, Truro

My Loves And Hates

I love it when it's thick and creamy.
I love it when the waves crash down and all the spray flies up.
I love it when the smell of freshly baked apple pie fills the room.
I love it when I go up that level.
I love it when I'm with that special person.
I love it when you just can't stop laughing.

I hate it when all the snow melts away.
I hate it when you get on the aeroplane home.
I hate it when you have to drag yourself out of bed.
I hate it when I'm not allowed out because of work the next morning.
I hate it when the sea is flat.
I hate it when the rain thumps down on the roof.

Josh Maloy (14)
Richard Lander School, Truro

I Love It When . . .

I love it when I chill out with my friends.
I love it when he smiles at me, secretly.
I love it when cows chomp on grass and wiggle their bums.
I love it when it's Friday and it's the beginning of a weekend.
I love it when people compliment me.
I love it when I spend most of the weekend on Facebook!

Chelsea Humby (13)
Richard Lander School, Truro

I Hate It When . . .

I love it when it rains when I'm in bed.
I love it when you have a beautiful view from your window.
I love being warm in bed, but can feel a light breeze.
I love it when he gives me long, warm hugs.
I love it when he says I look good with no make-up on.
I love it when you can smell turkey on Christmas morning.
I hate it when you can't trust people.
I hate it when you're sunbathing and someone flicks sand on you.
I hate it when my fringe doesn't fall right.
I hate it when you're playing COD and people kill you.
I hate it when my phone has no signal.
I hate it when you doubt me.

Chloe Sobey (14)
Richard Lander School, Truro

The Things I Love

I love it when the sun is hot,
I love it when I sit next to the fire,
I love it when it snows,
I love it when the waves sparkle,
I love it when the school is closed,
I love it all the time, day and night.

Jonathan Russell (12)
Richard Lander School, Truro

Winter, Summer And Presents

I love it when summer comes along,
I love it when the cold months come along,
I love it when I look out the window and snow is like crystals,
I love it when I see your face smiling whilst you unwrap the present I got you,
I love it when you sit there unwrapping presents,
I love it when the cold months go and I know the warm months are on their way!

Paige Brown (12)
Richard Lander School, Truro

My Best Friend

I love it when I see my best friend
I love it when she's happy and smiles
I love it when she laughs
I love it when me and her share secrets
I love her hair in the morning when it's fuzzy
I love it when I'm around her.

Courtney Smith (12)
Richard Lander School, Truro

My Perfect Day

I love it when I am in the sea
I love it when I am the only one in the sea
I love it when I get out the sea and I am cold, then I get in the shower
I love it when it snows like icing on a cake
I love it when I am in Portugal
I love it when it's hot like an oven.

Dylan Pina-Hoblyn (12)
Richard Lander School, Truro

Simply The Best

I love it when the surf is good
I love it when there's morning dew
I love it when I'm with my mates at school
I love it when it snows quite softly
I love it when there's no homework and when it's time to play
I love it when you smell fresh hay.

Louis Downing (12)
Richard Lander School, Truro

I Am Shocked

I am
The girl that's just been slapped
The bike racer just been lapped
The angry mum with a naughty daughter
The boy that read the news that covered slaughter.

I am
The angry person with a dent in their car
The boy that just saw a shooting star
The angry dad with a naughty child
The stupid boy with his record filed.

I am
The man that looked at the weather
He ordered a cotton sofa but it ended up as leather
The footballer that just scored a goal
Angry that it first hit the pole.

Amelia Ebanks (12)
St Bede's RC Middle School, Redditch

Happy I Am

I am
The smiling face
In the sun
The athlete
With the fastest run
The race car
That always speeds away
The flowers
That blossom in April and May
The library book
That everyone opens to read
A new puppy
With a brand new lead.

Kieran Kite (12)
St Bede's RC Middle School, Redditch

Scared I Am

I am
The nightmare that you can't escape from
The shadows that creep from door to door as you lay in bed
The broken old clown hanging and dead.

I am
The never-ending Friday the 13th that makes you paranoid
The creaking floorboard that keeps you awake
The ghost that plays with elucidations in dark corridors.

I am
The dark figures that slowly move towards you as you toss and turn
The transparent silhouette that gleams in the full moon's beam
The fright of Hallow's Eve as the dark rain cloud haunts your fear.

I am
The translucent grey cloud that flattens your failures
The addictive beam that carries you to the devastation of your past
The deepest secret exploding through your mind.

I am what you feel
Alone!

Jaynaya Cox (12)
St Bede's RC Middle School, Redditch

In Love I Am

I am
The tingle running down my spine
As he grasps my hand softly.
The adrenaline rushing through my veins
At the first kiss.
The romantic movie we saw
On our first date.

I am the heartbeat
Of the baby growing inside me.
The snuggliness of his jacket
As he wraps it round me warmly.
Juliet
Who has found her Romeo.

I am
The security I feel
Whenever I'm with him.
The butterflies in my stomach
As he presses his lips against mine.
The lyrics
To our love song.

I am
The remembrance of the day
When my eyes met his.
The amazing feeling I get
When I wake up and see him lying next to me.
The perfect rose
He searched miles to find.

Ellie Brown (13)
St Bede's RC Middle School, Redditch

I Am

I am
The three lions
Standing tall on the England badge,
The baby
Taking its first huge steps,
The aggressive cheetah's
First giant catch,
The ball
Entering victoriously into the goal at the World Cup Final.

I am
The new life,
Taking its first deep breath,
The Earth's
First spin,
The fizz
Bubbling in the gleaming can,
The first glimpse
Of the shining sun.

I am
The page
In the new, open book,
The A*
On the crystal white paper,
The bubble wrap
Making its first ear-splitting pop,
The groom
Saying, 'I do.'

Niall Lindsey & Kelan Hawkeswood
St Bede's RC Middle School, Redditch

160

Scary I Am

I am
The lonely boy
On his first day at school
The little girl
Hearing noises in the dark
The nervous girl
About to start her exams

I am the dark wolf
Howling at the moon
The creak
From the middle of the night
The immaculate knife
Shining from the other side of the door

I am
The deserted boy
Walking down the dark alleyway
The dark man
Coming to get you
The lonely girl
Listening to the rain and thunder outside

I am
The clown's face
Popping out of the dark
The email
Delivering the threat
The terrifying soundtrack
To the new horror film.

William Harris (12)
St Bede's RC Middle School, Redditch

Humiliated Am I

I am
The clown
When the hurtful joke didn't work
The small child who didn't understand the work set

I am
The driver who didn't understand the complicated map
The small boy who didn't understand the work set
The boy who couldn't do some of the skill the better players could
The model who tripped on the catwalk

I am
The adult who lost a huge job opportunity
The child who forgot his words in the huge assembly
The child who fell off the big chair
The chef who sent a poor meal and then got told off

I am
The girl who fell into the boy's toilet
The boy who was told off in front of the whole school.

Liam Smith (12)
St Bede's RC Middle School, Redditch

Hyper I Am

I am,
The smile
On the young children's faces,
As they wake up on Christmas morning.
The young, teenage boy,
Eagerly waiting for the FIFA 11 game to be released.
The young child
Who has just munched a tube of Smarties.

I am,
The tiny, brown hamster,
Crazily running around his cage.
The new, fluffy, brown puppy
Barking restlessly.
The little cat,
Chasing his owner for some liver.

I am,
The brightly coloured helium balloons,
Making people giggle and squeal everywhere.
The bright red, bouncy ball,
Bouncing higher than the clouds.
The shiniest silver Mini,
Being driven for the first time.

I am,
The cold can of Coke,
Waiting for someone to drink my fizz.
The beady eyeballs,
Gradually growing bigger and bigger, like my smile.
The fizzy champagne,
Ready to explode.

Mollie Louise Ralph (12)
St Bede's RC Middle School, Redditch

Angry I Am

I am,
The lightbulb,
Flickering constantly.
The boy,
Whose ice cream fell on the floor.
The car,
That's just been overtaken.
The hunter,
With an empty trap.

I am,
Raging, like a bear,
As red as an apple.
The steam,
Pumping out of the fireman's ears.
The dog,
Whose bone's just been stolen.
The girl,
Whose pencil's just snapped.

I am,
The bull,
Charging with *anger!*
The snap,
Of the crocodile's teeth.
The roar,
From the lion's mouth.
The victim,
Waiting for revenge.

Whitney Harris (12)
St Bede's RC Middle School, Redditch

Scared I Am

I am
The ticking clock
Echoing through the house
The tree branch
Poking at the window of the pitch-black room
The horror TV shows
I watch all the time

I am
My old teacher
With the mouldy teeth and the non-moving hair
The child
That's only two seconds away from being hit by a bus
The wind
Howling through the creepy night

I am
The child who has a reason not to get his football
From the old man's garden
The six-year-old joining a martial arts class
The baby
Taking its first steps
And thinking he will fall over

I am
The victim
Who sees the bully walking towards him
The student
Leaving for university
The seven-year-old
Who hasn't done his homework.

Rebecca Jones [12]
St Bede's RC Middle School, Redditch

I Am Angry

I am
A fiery volcano
Ready to erupt
A vicious dog
Ready to snap
A killer bear
Ready to kill

I am
A big rhino
Ready to spike someone with my horn
A young person
Ready to bellow at an old man
A bloodthirsty killer
Ready to kill

I am
An orange and black tiger, ready to pounce
A grey elephant ready to stomp on you
A green monster ready to eat you
A camouflaged soldier on the front line
A dog ready to go on a walk
A funny clown, ready to be pied in the face.

Seamus Townsend (12)
St Bede's RC Middle School, Redditch

In Love I Am

I am,
The beautiful swan,
Swimming freely on the water,
The elegant violin,
Whose sweet sound is standing out in the music.

I am,
The stunning rose petals,
That float around the warming bath,
As the beautiful music is played,
The sweet jokes you tell,
Which make me laugh, even when you're not with me.

I am,
The handsome bodyguard,
That stands tall and proud, outside the night-club,
The heart,
That beat 10,000,000 beats a minute,
When I see your face.

I am,
The mistletoe,
That hangs above your door on Christmas Day,
The beaming face,
When I saw you for the first time.

I am,
In love.

Georgia Smyth]12]
St Bede's RC Middle School, Redditch

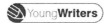
Hyper I Am

I am
The bubbles
In a fizzy cola can
The fires
Leaping from tree to tree
The excited and scared puppy
That you just bought home

I am
The newborn baby life
Welcomed into the world at night
The newly-turned vampire
Running for their first feed
The new star player in a rugby team
Who scores all the goals

I am
The little girl
Running downstairs on Christmas Day
A brand new reindeer
On its first flight over snowy London
A little child
Eating their first ice cream

I am
The bubbly personality
Within me
Very hyper
Me.

Nicole Sutton (12)
St Bede's RC Middle School, Redditch

Lonely Am I

I am
The lost lion cub
Searching for his mum
The newborn kitten
Searching for a home
The old, hungry dog
Wishing to be loved
The child
Who has no friends to play with

I am
The jumper that no one wants to wear
The new trainers that are full of dust
The old, dusty box which no one needs to use
The newly bought book that no one wants to read

I am
The colourful pen
Which has no ink, but is never refilled
The old boat
That was once loved, but never will be again
The fluffy hamster
Which you forgot to clean out
The purple pencil case
Which you forgot to use.

Annabelle Johnstone (12)
St Bede's RC Middle School, Redditch

In Love I Am

I am
The beautiful Juliet
As she finally meets her Romeo
The lyrics
To your favourite love song.

I am
Your beating heart, as he kisses you for the first time
And says goodnight
The heartbeat
Of a newborn baby.

I am
The notes
Your admirer sends
The butterflies
In your stomach.

I am
The mistletoe
Hanging above you on Christmas Day
The beautiful swan
Swimming freely in the water.

I am
The heartbeat
Of a newborn baby
The luscious lips
That you kissed on your second date.

I am
The fast beating heart
On your nervous first date
The fingers running through your hair.

Emily Blakemore (12)
St Bede's RC Middle School, Redditch

Irritating I Am

I am,
The alarm clock that
Wakes you up every day,
The feeling of the opposition
Scoring and celebrating
In your face,
The teacher telling you
To tie your lace.

I am,
The person eating crisps
So loudly you can't
Look away,
The brother who thinks he
Knows best,
When you come last in
Laser Quest.

I am,
The boring maths teacher
Droning on and on,
When you've had a bad dream
And can't get back to sleep,
A flat tyre
When you don't have a spare in the back.

I am,
Your car alarm going off
During your party,
When you try your best
And don't succeed,
When you try
But can't grow
A sunflower seed.

Owen Wiseman (12)
St Bede's RC Middle School, Redditch

Angry

I am
A bullied victim
About to get revenge
A bull charging at a
Red rag
The hard businessman
Who's stuck in traffic
After a long day.

I am
A tiger
Hunting for my food
The caveman
Trying to find shelter.

I am
The boy
That has just broken
His leg in a football match
The soldier
That has just watched his mate get killed.

I am
The military
That has just lost the
The swimmer
Who has just lost her
£50.00 swimming goggles.

Owen Boggis (12)
St Bede's RC Middle School, Redditch

London

The
Constant
Descants
And
Paroxysms of business
Saturating the streets
The parp of the black cab
And the bus
And the clapping
And slapping of the shoes
Of fashionistas and city bankers
And other
Jargons
Of
Zoom
Clink
And the harsh
Schhhhh
Crescendo of the road
The blah-blah-blah
Of the swarms of people
Clicking-clacking
On their phones;
Laconic replies to whomever -
Combining to make a monster
A monster
Bellowing in your ears;
Obstreperous and
Launching a scurrilous sound attack on you
Never-ending chaos
Always bustling;
The music of
London.

Hannah El-Hawary (13)
St Michael's Catholic Grammar School, London

Peeping Tom Goes Blind

Thanks to Lady Godiva,
We might not have to pay tax.
She'll be riding past my window,
I might get a look perhaps.

Lady Godiva is religious,
Unlike her husband, the Earl,
Maybe I could be her husband
And buy her a silver pearl.

I stand there, staring,
I just cannot resist,
She is so pretty,
Don't you get the gist?

This time she is in her birthday suit,
I know what I'm going to do,
Take a peep out the window,
Just for a minute or two!

So the day comes,
When Lady Godiva will ride past.
I'll prepare myself for her presence,
I better look good and fast!

My heart is beating,
I can't wait for the moment now.
Here she comes,
I can only say, 'Wow!'

Lifting up the curtains,
Gently as can be.
Will she be there?
I can't wait to see.

Her beautiful hair,
As golden as the sun,
Poised on her horse,
This is so much fun!

But then, oh so suddenly,
I can not see a thing!
Is this the work of a witch?
Oh no, what could life bring?

So now I live in darkness,
After my selfish peeping.
I spend my time fumbling around,
Just weeping and weeping.

Sorcha Leavey (11)
St Michael's Catholic Grammar School, London

What War Is To Me

The Tank
It stomps through the land,
Gobbling up miles, leaving only dust,
Firing mercilessly,
Its only use is shielding soldiers from danger.

Death
It devours innocent lives with ease,
A thief, stealing people, never to be seen again,
It's like a rhino flattening anything in its path,
A serial killer, murdering whoever it pleases,
Over and over again.

War
He breaks people into units,
A bug nibbling away at hope, trust and happiness,
Eating every crumb of peace,
Like a child with a muffin.

Bullet
It leaves only smoke and rubble,
Killing unsuspecting goodness,
Robbing, snatching lives,
A minute rocket spinning in the air,
Fighting for both sides,
No loyalty to anyone.

Gun
A neutral, evil weapon,
Releasing it's mean, killing children,
. . . a bullet.

Rebecca Tyrrell (11)
St Michael's Catholic Grammar School, London

How Could He

Tears softly slid down my cheek,
As I watched him leave,
I couldn't help but feel bleak,
He felt nothing for me.

I sat in bed all night, pondering,
I really couldn't sleep,
I kept thinking, *what is he wondering?*
I knew that he would soon forget me.

How could he do this to me?
I couldn't get him out of my head,
Why did he leave me? What could it be?
How long was he with her? Was it because of me?

He left three days ago now,
He must have been pleased,
I told myself I didn't care, he was a cow,
He'd been using me just for my money.

But the way that he told me was worse,
It was my special '31',
I think I will pause on this verse,
But I wouldn't let it hurt.

I always thought what we had was love,
I guess that I need to look on,
I guess that love is up above,
I didn't intend on finding another love.

My heart would pound,
Every time I saw a man,
I thought he was the one that I had found,
But they all walked by.

Love should come soon,
But now I am prepared,
I think this as I look up at the moon,
But I will not have my heart ripped apart.

Miriam Yemane (11)
St Michael's Catholic Grammar School, London

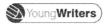

Who Let The Cat Out Of The Bag

I always wanted a pet,
But my parents always said no.
My mum said If I got a pet
She'd hang me by the toe.

One summer's holiday,
Before school began,
I went to buy a backpack,
On my own, because I can.

I searched through all the aisles,
From row one to twenty,
I did not want a single bag,
Even though there were plenty.

Then, suddenly, I saw it,
In aisle twenty one,
A bright, lime green rucksack,
I knew my shopping was done.

At home I zipped it open;
To check out all its space,
But out leapt a tabby cat
And it hung onto my face.

I showed my parents the kitten,
Their hearts melted right there.
I asked if I could keep him,
Then they nodded their heads and hair.

Now my kitten's older,
He's ours, with collar and tag,
I never forgot how I got him,
That's why he's called Handbag!

Kathryn O'Connell (11)
St Michael's Catholic Grammar School, London

The Last Kiss Of A Butterfly

I close my eyes
And she is standing right beside
She is here
She is with me in my dreams
She's with me
She didn't leave me
She didn't die
She survived
The cancer didn't take her away
She lived.

Beth Asante (11)
St Michael's Catholic Grammar School, London

Poem

Poems don't always have to rhyme
On every single line
But if you do it that way
It's bound to sound okay
And so it will turn out fine.

I wrote this little ditty
Because it makes me sound witty
But when I read it back
It has a certain lack
Of making sense.

So now it's the end
If this dead end
Goodbye for now
I'm off to milk the cow!

Holly Donnell (12)
St Osmund's CE (Aided) Middle School, Dorchester

Just Waves

Waves sprint across the ocean,
Breaking on the beach,
A flurry of snow-white horses
Disintegrate on the sandy shore.

The gentle whoosh of the ocean
Calling back the broken waves,
Crashing together,
Forming one once more,
Forever more they hope.

Separation again
And again,
For eternity,
Forever.

Waves sprint across the ocean,
Breaking on the beach,
A flurry of snow-white horses
Disintegrate on the sandy shore.
Then the whoosh
Calling them back,
Calling . . .

Lauren Steele (12)
St Osmund's CE (Aided) Middle School, Dorchester

Me And The Seasons

Summer
When it starts to grow hot
And the tourists arrive,
You know that summer is alive
And that big, red beach ball bounces off your head,
Your mother's screaming, 'Time for bed!'

Autumn
When the leaves grow old
And drift to the ground,
You know that autumn is around
And those spiky shells fall on your head,
The shiny conkers are in bed.

Winter
When the world turns white
And snow drifts down,
You know that winter is around
And that freezing snowball splats on your head,
But you still want to snooze in bed.

Spring
When the flowers bloom out
And the green leaves arrive,
You know that spring is alive
And the first few raindrops, drip, drop on your head,
Nature has got out of her bed!

Grace Osborne (11)
St Osmund's CE (Aided) Middle School, Dorchester

A Day In The Life Of Me

Have you ever asked yourself
What an eleven-year-old's life is like?
Here is a day in the life of me.

Seven am,
A screech in my ear,
A knock on the door,
'Oh, wake up dear.'

In my comes my bro,
Eight years old,
Jumps on my belly,
Shouts, 'Go, go, go!'

Hop down the stairs,
Missing a shoe,
Phone rings,
Friend asks,
'How are you?'

Mum shouts,
'Honey, you're gonna be late.'
Walk out the door,
I see my mate.

We run to school,
First lesson's in sports hall,
Run around the track,
Teach says, 'Come on you miserable lot,
Don't you slack!'

Second lesson's science,
Miss says, 'Today we'll work in silence.'
Third lesson,
What a flurry,
DT is such a hurry!

Fourth and fifth are both the same,
French, with Madame,
Boring Jane.

Lesson six and then the seventh,
In RE we talked about our vision of Heaven.
Lesson eight and nine are great -
English with Miss Garvy.

Find my friend,
Walk to the school gate,
Get home, Mum questions,
'What did you do in English today?
I reply, 'Poetry.'

Snuggle into bed,
Stomach filled with dread,
I forgot to do my homework,
It's to write this up in best!

Lucy Bone (11)
St Osmund's CE (Aided) Middle School, Dorchester

Ozzies

I belong to St Osmund's School,
I see it as a great learning tool.

The education I receive
Will help me in all that I can achieve.

To top it off, we have great staff,
Who make our lessons such a laugh.

So here are the teachers, one and all,
To help you make your way through school.

Our year eight tutor is Mrs Boon,
Who registers us morning and afternoon.

The school mathematician is Mr T,
Who will point out rules and strategies.

Mr Rooke is our PE teacher,
Out of school he is the store house preacher.

Now for a person I really like lots,
Teaching assistant Mr Watts.

Mrs Ryan, we all adore,
Although she cried at 'Carrie's War'.

An RE Lesson with Mrs Stevens,
Is guaranteed to be fair and even.

Another great teacher is Mr Beet,
Who expects homework tidy and neat.

Mr Pontin will give you a song,
Teaching music all day long.

Happy, nice, as busy as a bee,
Here is Mrs Roberts to coach rugby.

Mr Bourne can be found in the science lab,
His crazy experiments are really quite fab.

We end with the teacher who has the last say,
Give it up for Mr J!

Lucy Harron (12)
St Osmund's CE (Aided) Middle School, Dorchester

The Four Seasons

The summer air is sweet like roses,
The atmosphere is peaceful, like night-time,
Birds sing like a choir, filling the world with their sweet voices.

All the leaves have fallen in rainbow colours,
The animals prepare to hibernate
And the days seem shorter as night falls faster.

Everything is a snowy white,
The air is cold as ice,
Woolly hats, gloves and scarves appear,
Christmas is near!

All the lambs bounce happily, like bouncy balls,
The flowers bloom, showing pretty faces,
The animals awaken with their new babies,
Everyone prepares for the next season.

Nikki Hills (12)
St Osmund's CE (Aided) Middle School, Dorchester

The Modern Walk

Walking along the streets isn't easy these days,
You can't walk for long without someone in your way.
Dodging the lamp posts is tiresome and tricky,
Also treading on chewing gum makes my shoes sticky.
The horrific noise of roadworks battle through your ear
And when you see a drunken man, you walk fast, with fear.
Forgetting about cigarettes and pot holes in the street,
Walking with lack of concentration you get dog poo on your feet.
Walking down the streets isn't easy these days,
There's a baby in a buggy - get out my way!

Hannah Smalldon (12)
St Osmund's CE (Aided) Middle School, Dorchester

The Ocean

Like a piece of jigsaw,
As blue as the sky,
It whispers in the wind,
As you go by.

Although it looks empty,
It is full of life,
You maybe will find
In some parts there is strife.

Like a desert it is far,
Like a country it is wide,
Just you watch
As these two things collide.

Jump on board,
Let's go for a ride,
Across the ocean.
You decide.

Shona Sealy (12)
St Osmund's CE (Aided) Middle School, Dorchester

Autumn

The shy autumn breeze struggles to pass through the trees,
It must have been weeks since the frost-covered grass
Had been stepped on last.
The heat given off by the fire,
Which sits next to hearth, leaves the cold leaves forming a path.
Houses stand bold when fighting off the bitter cold.
When staring at the clear sky, birds can be seen flying so high.
Halloween closes in, leaving everything very dim.
Remember, remember the fifth of November,
One match can make a shower of fireworks
And leave your clothes smelling like smoke the next morning,
When autumn has gone you only have one year
Until the next autumn cheer.

Emma Murgatroyd (12)
St Osmund's CE (Aided) Middle School, Dorchester

A Country Walk

The tinged brown of the fading summer sun,
The glistening water swirling round my wellies,
Sasha, my dog, tugging strenuously on the lead,
Jumping into the water, paddling in circles like an excited child,
Dark pools of water rippling slowly downstream,
Sheep grazing relentlessly on the grass,
Yellow, orange and brown autumn leaves clinging hopefully to the branch,
Birds tweeting and chirping happily in the distance,
Ruby red berries hanging like jewels in the autumn sunlight,
The heady scent of pink Himalayan river flowers engulfs me,
Swoosh, as the autumn leaves are blown to the woodland floor,
The chilling water gushing down the rapids,
Diamonds encrusted on the waves as they hurtle onwards,
River reeds rustling on the riverbank,
The sun setting in the west,
A thousand rays of sunshine falling asleep,
This is my country walk!

Lucy Walker (12)
St Osmund's CE (Aided) Middle School, Dorchester

The True Meaning Of Christmas

It's the 24th of December.
Time to celebrate that we're Brits,
Sadly, I'm having no fun,
Cos I'm scared out of my wits.

Some say that he's 900lb,
Which means that he's obese,
He'll sneak inside of your house
And on your food he'll feast!

Waiting by the fireplace,
With my baseball bat,
If he comes down our chimney
I'll surely beat him flat!

Slowly down he slithers,
He's not very frisky
And in a very low-pitched voice
He asks me, 'Where's the whiskey?'

It is when he is munching,
When I punch him with my fist,
Letting out a huge cry
He says I'm on the naughty list!

Santa left that evening,
Flew back to the North Pole,
Sadly, next Christmas,
I'm not looking forward to coal!

Jack Davies (12)
St Osmund's CE (Aided) Middle School, Dorchester

Autumn's Dream

Leaves fluttering like butterflies in the wind,
Crimson, browns and golds,
I try to catch the falling leaves,
Drifting down from the trees.

Soon these trees will be bare
And ugly, like skeletons.
I watch a squirrel run up a tree trunk
And leap and fly through the fallen leaves,
A smile spreads across my lips.

As the sun goes down and the stars come out,
The moon hangs in the air, beaming.
The trees begin to whisper
About secrets I can't understand.

As I kick up fallen leaves with my boots,
A deer, running into the clearing
With its graceful lopes,
It's coat the colour of autumn.

Autumn's kiss holds the air,
Freezes the world in time,
The trees sigh,
This is autumn.

Eilish Hart (12)
St Osmund's CE (Aided) Middle School, Dorchester

The Final Whistle

The ref blew, contact begun
I broke my bones, nobody won
We tried so hard, he scored a try
Then I was tackled, he made me cry

We ran forwards, he lost his boot
But someone still shouted, 'Shoot!'
The ball was in the net, what a goal
But the three points they stole

My racquet was as hard as steel
But still I was losing, 30-nil
He was amazing, played me off the court
However hard I fought

The goggles were smiling with teeth
Even though I was beaten by Keith
I was tired, I huffed and puffed
And had indigestion because I was stuffed

Its' the end of an amazing day
Time to go home and play
Though I was disappointed with what the score line showed
When the final whistle blowed.

Jack Cartwright (12)
St Osmund's CE (Aided) Middle School, Dorchester

Autumn

The birds sing their songs,
The leaves turn red, yellow, orange and gold.
The heating goes on,
The fluffy hats appear.

The true sign of autumn.

The animals snuggle up together,
The leaves fall to the ground.
It's dark at 6pm,
The scarves keep us warm.

The true sign of autumn.

The trees go bare,
The houses light up.
The gloves keep our hands warm,
The migrating birds leave us.

The true sign of autumn,

The very true sign of autumn.

Catherine Simmons (12)
St Osmund's CE (Aided) Middle School, Dorchester

Autumn

Autumn is . . .

The crunchy leaves fallen from trees,
The chilly, grumbling, gusty breeze.
Conkers pickled for the conker fights,
Bonfires roaring for firework night.

Misty mornings, moonlit skies,
Squirrels scamper, while barn owl flies,
Dormice and hedgehogs making their nests,
Storing away food, ready for their rest.

First frosty morning, cold breath in the air,
Trees shed their leaves, their branches are bare.
Toadstools emerging, from the leaf-strewn ground,
Pumpkins for Halloween, orange and round.

Toffee apples to enjoy on Bonfire Night,
Pumpkin lanterns, carved and burning bright.
Leaves changing colour, like a traffic light,
All to show that winter is in sight.

Anabel Mitchem (13)
St Osmund's CE (Aided) Middle School, Dorchester

Summer

The golden, glistening sun shines down on me,
Walking slowly, I can feel the sand running through my toes.
Crashing loudly against my legs
The blue shimmering waves tower above me,
With the wild, whistling wind blowing me like a feather.

Looking above, the stony cliffs are crumbling over my head.
With birds gliding around them and scavenging for food,
Like there's no tomorrow.
Families around me eating picnics and playing with their dogs,
The children making sandcastles and jumping over waves.

Breathing in, all I can smell is salt,
The sweet smell of the glowing, blue sea.
The warmth of summer all around me,
The summer has come round once again.

Chloe Neil (12)
St Osmund's CE (Aided) Middle School, Dorchester

The Monster

Creaking and squeaking, a whisper in the night
When it comes for you it will give you a fright
Lying in bed, waiting for dawn
Can't close my eyes until the morn

Opening my wardrobe door
Looking around the bedroom floor
Searching underneath my bed
Oh, maybe it's all just in my head!

Robert Adams (12)
St Osmund's CE (Aided) Middle School, Dorchesteruntitled

Just think of this,

Hundreds of bits of metal,
Put them together in a certain way,
Add some oil here and there,
Then fill with fuel.

Pull a lever and those bits start to move.
Whirring and stirring,
Pushing, pulling and sometimes banging,
Connect them up to a chassis and wheels,
Something magical starts to happen,
The wheels start to turn.

Inside the lump of metal,
Well-oiled pistons are turning well-oiled cylinders,
Bright blue, electric sparks ignite crystal clear fuel.

A beautiful thing is an engine.

Joss Minterne (12)
St Osmund's CE (Aided) Middle School, Dorchester

The Sky Teacher

The sky is a great big teacher.
One day her smile will beam warmth down on us,
But the next day she's like a dark, grey cloud of gloom,
Raining on all of us, darkening our day.
Her eyes are made of ice, freezing us all,
But when she smiles we smile too.

Sam Dance (11)
St Osmund's CE (Aided) Middle School, Dorchester

Teacher Says

Teacher says we have to write a poem,
Don't know what to do, but I really wanna show him
That I can do it,
That I can do it.
Sitting, staring, looking at the screen,
Writing poems, I'm really not that keen,
I have to do it,
I have to do it.
Yes! I've got it, I know what to do,
Gonna write a rap and I'm gonna write it soon.
Yes, I did it!
Yes, I did it!

Fricka, fricka,
Fresh!

Ellie Smith (12)
St Osmund's CE (Aided) Middle School, Dorchester

Taz

I've got a dog called Taz, we think he's about four
He's got a lot of bad habits
Like scratching his bum on the floor
He tries so hard to listen, to everything you say
But unless it involves food, he'll ignore you anyway
He's got his own language, it's like he tries to talk
When I get home from school, I take him for a walk
He sits up at the window and watches the world go by
He barks at the people and still we wonder why
I know he can't be with me 'til I'm one-hundred and eleven
But I know he'll be OK, 'cause all dogs go to heaven.

Leah Dear (12)
St Osmund's CE (Aided) Middle School, Dorchester

To my Dearest Love

Your love is the key to my happiness,
I need you every day.
Be by my side forever,
Oh, why can't it be that way?
I fall to pieces whenever we kiss,
Your eyes sparkle like the stars above,
Being together is the biggest thing I miss,
I cannot explain my passionate love.

Why are you at war again?
The place where you only feel pain.
Please come back home to me,
Because you're driving me insane.
We go back to the days
Where we could watch TV
And where we snuggle up together,
This would mean the world to me.

So please, come home to me now
And stay by my side,
I love you so much,
It's something I just can't hide.

From
The girl that misses you.

PS - I love you.

Rachel Smith (13)
St Osmund's CE (Aided) Middle School, Dorchester

Love

Long lasting love
That seeps from the heart,
As sweet as a flower,
Like some kind of art.

Friendship between two pulsing hearts,
Never can be broken
As long as it lasts.
The joy it can bring to everyone's soul,
Something to cherish,
Like reaching your goals.
It leads you onward,
Through night and through day.
The best feeling ever,
Anyone would say.

Ellen Porter (12)
St Osmund's CE (Aided) Middle School, Dorchester

The Fifth Of November

The dark, silent night,
The trees whisper,
The fire replies,
But not a sound is heard in the silent awaiting.
Then they come,
Screaming, shouting,
Shedding their beautiful lights,
As they are shot into the darkness,
Exploding in the sky,
A flying flurry of flames,
Lighting up the dark,
Flashes, crackles, whizzes and bangs fill the air
And then . . .
Back to silence.

Liam Churchill (12)
St Osmund's CE (Aided) Middle School, Dorchester

Army Of The Past

Grey and bleak all round,
Nothing there, but that double beat sound.
Infinite darkness consumes the light,
They all get ready for that bloodlust fight.

Warriors, failing to defeat the game,
All in agony of noxious pain.

They step out, every one,
They look down for armour; there is none.
The darkness spreads without a doubt,
Every face with an awesome pout.

Warriors, failing to defeat the game,
All in agony of noxious pain.

Now the men spread like army ants.
With that sickly feeling that adrenaline plants.
Swords are raised, then swung down fast,
All this because of an old, dead past.

Warriors, failing to defeat the game,
All in agony of noxious pain.

Shields uplifted, mercy cries,
With earnest belief each man tries
To win a battle that is already lost,
The end is nigh and the coin is tossed.

Esther Kagi (11)
St Osmund's CE (Aided) Middle School, Dorchester

High Spirits

Buoyant and alert,
He charged towards his goal.
Nose to the ground,
Oblivious to all around him.

Further and further
The scent took him,
Until there stood the deer,
Proud and elegant.

Trees gave shelter to the deer,
The puppy miles away,
But still he kept running,
Until all hope was gone.

In defeat,
He lay down on the ground,
But before long
Something caught his eye.

Round and round he chased his tail,
Like a swirling whirlwind,
Flying through the frosty air,
Not a care in the world.

Poppy Hosford (11)
St Osmund's CE (Aided) Middle School, Dorchester

The Poem

I've been thinking all night
But it doesn't sound right,
My poem won't come to me
The right words all flee.
For a poem is a lovely thing
In which all the right words sing,
They form up in a line
And some of them rhyme.
They march with a beat
Which is quite a great feat
And they say more than those
Words arranged just in prose.
I fear now you know it -
I'm really no poet!

John Reedie (12)
St Osmund's CE (Aided) Middle School, Dorchester

Environment

The countryside is radiant
The trees are swaying in the joyful breeze
The grass is growing
Life is coming
The birds are humming
The wolves are howling
The mice are scratching
The wasps are buzzing
The farmers are picking
The spiders are weaving
The night is coming
The day is going
Shhh, the countryside is sleeping.

Hannah Wyatt (12)
St Osmund's CE (Aided) Middle School, Dorchester

Poem

In the future you will see
Hover cars for you and me
Trips to the moon
You just wait, it will be here soon

Red sky loaded with radiation
People thinking it's an illusion
Crawling for underground vaults
Like young, frisky colts
Huge buildings with advanced technology
And new cures with our biology

Don't think it's all a walk in the park
It may become really dark, but . . .
In the future you will see
The advantages for you and me!

Dan Davies (12)
St Osmund's CE (Aided) Middle School, Dorchester

My Pet

I have a cat called Smudge,
He has loads of fur,
He loves to purr,
I also have six ferrets,
There are four boys and two girls,
They are just getting a winter coat,
Ready for the snow,
They'll be skiing soon!

Melissa Merritt (12)
St Osmund's CE (Aided) Middle School, Dorchester

Soldiers

Why do soldiers fight?
They give their lives,
When they die they see the light,
But not their wives.

They use the guns,
In their uniform,
They never see their sons,
They need to fight in a snowstorm.

They give poppies to the people who have died,
Lay on the ground,
People cried,
No sound.

Dan Thomson (12)
St Osmund's CE (Aided) Middle School, Dorchester

Wonders Of The World

Rainforest, letting out a weary cry
Asking you to help it before it dies
Children giving a deafening whine
When their favourite pet has died
All the wonders of the world destroyed.

The pollution and ignorance of fellow chums
Should think a lot more on what they've done
The chopping of trees, the greenhouse gases
Are killing animals in their masses
All the wonders of the world destroyed

Destroying animals, destroying trees
Causing pollution, killing bees
Nature is getting locked away
Never to see the light of day
All the wonders of the world destroyed.

Laura Barrett (11)
St Osmund's CE (Aided) Middle School, Dorchester

Fireworks

Bang, crash, whizz, go the fireworks above me,
The ash of the firework sparkles on my shoulder.
Catherine wheels spinning round and round,
I start getting sick and dizzy,
My mum goes to get some candyfloss,
It feels like sparklers, alive in my mouth.

Time to set of all the rockets,
'Yippee!' shout the children from behind me.
My dad kneels down in front of me,
He takes the lighter in his hand.
The heat is getting hotter,
Whizz goes the rocket,
Bang goes the firework.
Everyone goes, 'Ooh, aah,' as they appear in the sky.

The bonfire is dying down,
Everyone sings campfire songs,
A jolly time is over,
We all say goodbye,
We all leave with smiles on our faces.

Georgia Mae Daw (12)
St Osmund's CE (Aided) Middle School, Dorchester

Autumn Leaves

In autumn, when the trees are brown,
The golden, little leaves come tumbling down.
They only make the slightest sound,
When the howling wind blows them to the ground.

But when autumn wind goes running,
It does some wild things.
It gives the shadows frightening figures
And makes the bright, crisp leaves sing.

Rebecca Hawkins (11)
St Osmund's CE (Aided) Middle School, Dorchester

Ride The Waves

The white horses gallop along the fields of the waves,
Rearing, tumbling and breaking, they gracefully play.
The quiet ones, shy and elegant, calmly rippling over the pebbles,
The fierce ones, bucking away the salty breeze
And crashing to the earth below.
Creeping behind you, here tsunami comes,
Cantering along, never breaking into a trot.
Helpless, you can never get away
Before the current pulls you under.
Fluffy and innocent they may seem,
But the swell is too much for young riders.

Flora Johnson (11)
St Osmund's CE (Aided) Middle School, Dorchester

Life Is A Tree

Life is a tree,
It twists and turns,
Nothing to control it.
The branches spread of their own accord,
Impossible to burn.

They stretch out with their open fingers,
Thinning at their tips,
The roots dig deep into the ground,
Standing safe in its home.
Its buds unfurl with growth and grace,
In bloom, their beauty glistens in the golden sun.

And as the summer season ends
Its grace and beauty
Falls into the winter snow.
The tree of life to be reborn,
The tree of life
Reborn to grow.

Aislin Fields (11)
St Osmund's CE (Aided) Middle School, Dorchester

In My World

Under my bed there's:
Bits of plastic
A lost sock
Maybe a magazine

An empty bottle
Clumps of dust
Maybe even some Plasticine

In my wardrobe there's:
A pair of jeans
A blue jumper
Also a hat

A T-shirt
Some shorts
Maybe even a sack

In my corridor there's:
A staircase
A rail too
Also a rack with shoes

A coat rack
An umbrella as well
Even some snooker cues

In my living room there's:
A sofa
A TV
And a stool

A dining table
A printer
A computer as well
(that's so cool!)

In my kitchen there's:
A microwave
A sink
And an oven

A cooker
A drying rack
Even a mum who's stubborn

That concludes my story of my world.

Ross Guy (12)
St Osmund's CE (Aided) Middle School, Dorchester

The Solider

In the depths of the mud-filled trench
The soldier awaits the signal,
For the Germans to take his short-lived life
And send him off to Heaven.

The signal is up,
Clutching his rifle, he gets up and runs.
His heart pounding in his ears,
The German guns are silent.

All is going well for him,
They are nearing the German lines,
The tops of the Germans' helmets are now in sight,
As they scurry back and forth.

The stony silence is shattered
By sudden machine gun fire.
Sprinting now,
His rifle firing for all that it's worth.

The line of soldiers is shredded,
Soldiers fall all around,
Their faces gripped with pain,
Bullets thud into him,
Finally he comes to rest, in the comfort of death.

Christopher Ninham (12)
St Osmund's CE (Aided) Middle School, Dorchester

The First Fallen

It's autumn,
The stage is set,
She tumbles gracefully from the old oak,
She; the first fallen.
Nobody watches her lonely descent,
Flitting and flying in glee.

It's autumn,
The season is in full flow.
Golden explosions of breathtakingly beautiful dancers,
Twirl down from the old oak tree.

Star-struck strangers stop to watch the spectacular whirlwind,
Busily leaping to the already covered floor.

It's autumn,
The final curtain has fallen.
Twisting and twirling
He silently spins down from the old oak -
He; the last fallen.

Ellie Chambers (11)
St Osmund's CE (Aided) Middle School, Dorchester

Comb Jelly

Gliding gracefully through the water of the deep
This little jewel silently seeks
To shine brighter than a star
And to bring light to the dark.

Behold in awe, it's shining folds
Glowing like neon and smoother than silk
As it gracefully glides through the water of the deep.

Trapping its prey like a net
It glides through water of the deep
All behold this little jewel
Behold in awe as it glides gracefully
Through the water of the deep.

Aldo D'Arrigo (11)
St Osmund's CE (Aided) Middle School, Dorchester

The Mists

Mist,
The ghost who walks the streets,
Whispering long-gone secrets.

Its tendrils sweeping, enclosing.
Obscuring.

Shadows looming - sounds muffled.

Drifting on the shifting winds,
Mists dance like cold ghost
On the frightened fields.

The magical, mysterious mists
Swallow up terrified towns.
Missssts!

Eloise Carter (11)
St Osmund's CE (Aided) Middle School, Dorchester

The Archer

As he straddles the line, the archer draws his bow,
Moulding the world around him to silence.
As he loses he hears the sweet music of an arrow in mid-flight,
Once more his ears smile as he hears the aimed
Middle-aged missile strike.

Out in the wood, the same man sees a deer,
He repeats his earlier moves; draw, aim, release.
With a mangled cry that deer then dies
And the man moves for his prize.

The following week the man goes to war
And fights the French, for respect and more.
On the battlefield he thinks of the days at the butts or in the forest
And copies his moves again; draw, aim, release.
He cries with joy as he hits a Frenchman.

He goes on like this for a day and a half,
But then a French cuts through his heart,
His final words are,
'Don't play God, or God will play you.'

Ben Macklin (11)
St Osmund's CE (Aided) Middle School, Dorchester

My Machines

Helicopters, helicopters, roaring with might
Helicopters, helicopters, bolts so tight
Helicopters, helicopters, never withold
Helicopters, helicopters, do as they're told,
Helicopters, helicopters, are unique
Helicopters, helicopters, never squeak

Tanks, tanks, never play pranks
Tanks, tanks, the top of the ranks
Tanks, tanks, never complain
Tanks, tanks, never mind the pain
Tanks, tanks, are mighty strong
Tanks, tanks, never wrong.

I love my machines!

Jordan Mitchell (11)
St Wilfrid's School, Exeter

What Matters To Me, Love Matters

Love matters to me.
I love my family,
I love my friends.
There is nothing else that is more important.

Love matters to me.
Love is a feeling and a thought,
Shown in words and actions,
Perhaps a kind word or a shoulder to cry on.

Love matters to me.
Love makes me feel so warm inside,
The feeling in your stomach is like a butterfly
Fluttering away.
You would feel so empty inside
Without any love.
Love is important, love matters.

Aja Humphries (12)
St Wilfrid's School, Exeter

Snow In The Wood

The wood had leaves scattered on the ground,
As they shone with the mixed
Red, yellow, blue and brown,
With shots of green.

But up in the sky, all white as wool,
Secrets are soon shared
As winter dawns.
White specks of diamond flutter down,
Falling light as a feather, but at its own pace,
Making up pillows of stars and trees.
Writing unknown words like
Bap, batombed, magpappins and mogs,
As they dance down like crystals,
Glowing as bright as lights.

Now in the wood all yellow and brown,
Icing is shimmering on trees,
The ice giant weaves a white,
Woolly raglan, woven out of magic
From a single bobbin.

Down it falls, onto the banks,
Someone's been dropping wool.
Glass towers dangle of ice,
Full of miniscule people inside.

Footprints appear like holes in paper,
Leading to peaceful spots.
As squirrels will run, rabbits will jump,
Punching more holes in the white.

In the trees a chorus of birds
Gather to sing in the choir,
Singing so sweet, so high, so pretty,
While underground, moles gather
To tell their children a ditty
Under the silent snow.

The wood is still, all quiet,
Apart from the deer playing tag,
As young squirrels play hide-and-seek
All over the wood.
The giant, bright sun shines down
Upon the crystal fleece.

Matthew Heathcote (12)
St Wilfrid's School, Exeter

The Stars Of My Dreams

The spring star looks so shiny
But ever so minute,
It looks upon an apple tree
And smiles down gleefully.

The summer star shines brightly
But only when it will,
It looks upon a cherry tree
That whistles in the breeze.

The autumn star looks lively
But never is so shiny,
It looks upon a Ja Ja tree
And sings out merrily.

The winter star is tiny
But still ever so mighty,
It looks upon a conifer
And glistens happily.

All the stars together
Look down upon the trees
And as I sleep I know that they
Guard the temple of my dreams.

Emily Piper (11)
St Wilfrid's School, Exeter

Animals

Feathers, scales, spikes and fur,
They squeak, tweet, roar and purr.

Floppy, pointy and curly tails,
Hopping rabbits and gooey snails.
Swinging from trees and flying high,
Some as fluffy as the clouds in the sky.

Pink, blue, green glassy eyes,
Slithering snakes go in disguise.

Big cats slinking in the shadows,
Fish all swimming in the shallows.

Spiky teeth and gentle faces,
Fast, slow and sluggish paces.

Dark, wet, sniffing noses,
Tails twist and sway like hoses.

Fireflies float like stars in the air,
Happy foals skip by a tired, old mare.

All these things are now in shapes,
Of lamps, rugs and coats of all makes.

Elephants lie without tusks or feet,
Lions are killed for fur and not meat.

The trees are chopped for the paper I use,
So many fur coats and scarves to choose.

Roots are ripped and leaves are torn,
Mounted on the wall is a cub or a fawn.

To help these things it is too late,
But who knows, we cannot predict our own fate.

Laura Wells (12)
St Wilfrid's School, Exeter

War

War is hurt
War is heartache
War is pain
War is deadly
War is Hell

War can kill
War can end the world
War can be harsh
War can be dangerous
War can be the end of lives

War is never Heaven
War is never flowers
War is never dead
War is never fun
War is always the Devil.

Make love not war!

James Dutton [13]
St Wilfrid's School, Exeter

My Pet

When I was six
I got a pet,
It was small,
Not big yet.

It doesn't drink much,
But likes to eat;
Lots of lettuce
But never meat.

He likes to climb
Steps and walls;
In the kitchen
And down the hall.

He's good at escaping -
He's got such a knack,
He's very random,
But he always comes back.

I once chucked him
Down a slide,
He didn't like it,
He almost died.

The strange pet that
My dad bought us
Is none other than
A tortoise!

Elliot Dawson (12)
St Wilfrid's School, Exeter

Love

Roses are red
Violets are blue
All you need to do is say I love you
Your face is like the sunrise

Daisies are yellow
Lilies are white
I love you day and night
In my dreams I see you

All my life and in my dreams
I have never come across you
I'll do anything you want me to
You're the sun on a sunny day

Love is what matters
If you love one another
You should be able
To love the whole world.

Deborah Adebola (12)
Sarah Bonnell School, Stratford

What Matters To Me

See the leaves that fall from trees
Watch them fall to the ground with grace
Carried by the winds of Nature
They never stay in just one place.

See the leaves that fall from trees
They grew from branches nice and quick
A season's when they have their life
Fall and shortly poisoned, sick.

See the leaves that fall from the trees
They're now swept up on the farm
Don't even let them have their last breath
Grounded, lifeless, no beauty at all.

Won't see the future of our kind
Our greed has brought is to our knees
We have condemned all forms of life
And drunk the water of the sea
We have no second Earth to hide
We had the care but no open eye
To see the leaves that fall from the trees.

See the leaves that fall from trees
The venom that we always show
We eradicate our own Mother Nature
And the life that flows through the air.

Nisha Kaur (11)
Sarah Bonnell School, Stratford

Visualise Poverty

Visualise a world where . . .
Hunger is a hunt,
Death is a familiar face,
Life is a hazard,
That's poverty!

Visualise a world where . . .
Support is needed, but who to look for?
Support is needed, but what to look for?
Money is an issue,
Thief is what you're called, Thief is your name,
That's poverty!

Visualise a world where . . .
Life is a roller coaster ride,
As the pain grows, life deteriorates,
As the roller coaster ride reaches out to you
You learn the world will not stand by you,
But you will stand by the world,
That's poverty!

Visualise a world where . . .
Wars are fought,
Earthquakes, floods, tsunamis occur frequently,
The tornado spins your mind tight round, until . . . *stop!*
Silence strikes and the world is given a farewell
That lasts *forever!*
That's poverty!

Shanjidah Ahad (12)
Sarah Bonnell School, Stratford

My Family

Families are the main roller coaster throughout life,
It has its ups, it has its downs,
Even if lightning strikes,
Even in the coldest days,
The ongoing train of my family
Goes on and on.

Each person in my family is a
Blossom on a tree,
Through winter and autumn,
Each blossom grows and grows,
Just like the love of my family,
Families are the main roller coaster throughout life.

Mythily Nagarajah (12)
Sarah Bonnell School, Stratford

Think About . . .

Family and friends
Help you to the end
Keep you safe and sound
No danger is around

Floods are sweeping the people
We need to make them equal
With all our help
We can give shelter.

Hanna Girma (11)
Sarah Bonnell School, Stratford

War . . . Death . . . And Closure

Closure is a very beautiful thing,
Without it; we are nothing.
Like a closed bud in the middle of spring,
Helpless . . . lifeless . . . useless.

Closure is needed for different things . . .
But mainly death.
The loss of someone is like walking with broken limbs,
Painful . . . difficult . . . impossible.

We all get over it - hopefully,
Slowly but surely.
It can be like a child eating wilfully,
Slow . . . hard . . . tiring.

War and death go hand in hand,
Of course they do.
It'd be like a beach with no sand,
Wrong . . . odd . . . weird.

You have to kill to win a war,
Or so they think.
Like drugs, they satisfy the urge to settle the score,
Murder . . . death . . . war.

We're recognised as numbers in their selfish blood battle,
Not the people that we are.
Rounded up and killed, just like beef cattle,
Quickly . . . steadily . . . eagerly.

Eager to see someone die,
That's just wrong.
Like throwing a baby into the sky,
Cruel . . . sick . . . evil.

Tyler Cormack (12)
Sarah Bonnell School, Stratford

Nothing

Global warming is breaking the ozone layer
And what are we doing about it?
Nothing
Cars are causing pollution
And what are we doing about it?
Nothing
Vandalism is causing fights
And what are we doing about it?
Nothing
Fights are causing crying
And what are we doing about it?
Nothing
Crying is causing deaths
And what are we doing about it?
Nothing
Death is causing sadness
And what are we doing about it?
Nothing
Nothing! Nothing! Nothing!

Nazia Rahman (12)
Sarah Bonnell School, Stratford

Creatures

Birds fly so high,
Up in the bright sky.
Cheetahs run super fast,
While snails come last.
Monkeys have a laugh,
As hippos take their bath.
Giraffes are very tall,
But I hope they don't fall.
Last but not least,
Let the creatures have their feast.

Sanjidah Chowdhury (11)
Sarah Bonnell School, Stratford

Close To My Heart

I love my family
Because they're caring
And always sharing
Their belongings
They look after me

My friends cheer me up
And always by my side
Whenever I need help
That's what friends are for

I like animals
But dogs are the best
I have a little puppy
He has a white chest
He is always on a quest.

Nicole Cook (11)
Sarah Bonnell School, Stratford

Family

Families are strong bonds that can never break if there is love.
Although they may annoy you,
They are the path that shows you the right path.
Mothers and fathers are worth more than gold,
I wouldn't have grown without their side,
Thank you Mum and Dad.

Even if I try to repay them
I would never be able to repay for what they've done for me,
No matter how hard I try.

When ever I have trouble, I have my family's shoulder to lean on.
Without their love I would never succeed.
I love my family.

Aamna Ali (12)
Sarah Bonnell School, Stratford

My Grandparents

Time flew by, I still think in my head
All my grandparents from this world you have fled.
Tears fall down, they make me drown,
When grey clouds turn brown, my smile turns to a frown.

Oh, how I wish you were here, close to me
So I could hold you in my arms, never set you free.
Oh, how I wish you were here sitting next to me
So I could show you all the things that you really need to see.

I know you're okay, because your soul's so pure
Lying up in Heaven, a place so secure.
I cannot live without your support
I remember how strong you were, how well you fought.

How much I miss you, you would never know
Oh, how much I crave that you could watch me grow.
Time flew by, but I still think in my head
All my grandparents from this world you have fled.

Afsana Begum (11)
Sarah Bonnell School, Stratford

What Matters To Me

W orld peace that makes the world go round
H appiness and smiles all around
A nd food for everyone, not hunger for any
T here are people who can't even spare a penny

M oney, that's the problem, no need to be greedy
A mazing people help the needy
T he Amazon and rainforest being cut down
T he poor animals scattering all around
E xcellent families helping each other
R espect and love one another, and
S ome people don't even matter

T rust in someone is everything
O pen hearts are definitely one thing

M ore to give to everyone
E very day life is more than just one!

Jumana Ahmed (11)
Sarah Bonnell School, Stratford

Cerulean Vision

If you ever find yourself haunted by strange visions,
Somewhere, in an unknown nation,
Then stop
And look around you.
For there are countless others
Who walk this land
And are going through the same ordeal.

If you ever find yourself in need of someone special,
Someone who can perceive your vision,
Then stop
And look deep inside yourself
For the is no other person
Who walks this land
And perceives the world with such eyes as your own.

Sakeen Zaman (15)
Sir John Cass Foundation & Red Coat School, London

Words Are More Than Actions

I'm sick of love's situation
What's the point of flying cupids when they lead to no gain?
An arrow not for romance but for infatuation
I won't wait in the rain
My self-control is shattering away
Nothing but heartless emotions are in my firing line
My patience is not going to stay
Now I'll make the outcome mine
Bitter-sweet coping
Words are more than actions
How can flowers bring such hoping?
I don't see this façade as a dissatisfaction
You should be glad I'm not ending this with a fight of who won
'Cos here thou has made me move on.

Tamanna Khanum (16)
Sir John Cass Foundation & Red Coat School, London

Women Of The World Unite

Women of the world
Where do we stand?
Or should I say kneel -
Before our masters

Women of the world
Where do we kneel?
Or should I say submit -
To our husbands

Women of the world
Where do we submit?
In our solitary confinement
Chastised by shackles and cages

Warmth from our irons
Comfort from our vacuums
Salvation from our cooking
Protection from our oppressors

Women of the world
When shall we fight?
To emancipate our sisters
From this tyranny of men.

Dilwar Hussain (17)
Sir John Cass Foundation & Red Coat School, London

Sojourn

She, in all her splendour, sits alone in the midst of a forest; staring through the jade green fringe
The icy breeze whispers something to the trees, making her cringe
Her mission tonight; to climb the starry skies
Leaving behind all the sorrow, the pain and all the lies
On a cloud she shall sit and watch the magnificent sphere turn
For this night is sojourn
Tomorrow she'll be looking at life through a telescope
Everything is so far, dreams and reality alike and with each passing day she loses hope
But not tonight. Tonight she consoles the mystical creatures on her journey
From therein they will be her attorney
Because they have the insight to her heart
If anyone else were to catch a glimpse they would think it to be a beautiful piece of art
Created to look like the ripples in a river,
Caused by the throwing of a rock
In her heart each ripple holds even more sadness;
it is this which has caused her to lock
It is at moments like this that she breaks the barriers which keep her tied down, like a red balloon tangled by angry seaweed
When she ponders matters similar to this the unicorns intercede
They fly her round the star-studded blanket;
The passing zephyr grasps hold of the thoughts and blows them away
It's hard to believe that the gaudy days and the mysterious night deny
The extent of this peacefulness and serenity
Though only a girl with an ingenious mind could generate a scene like that; a nonentity
But that was just the problem;
It was her imagination.

Nazifa Begum (15)
Sir John Cass Foundation & Red Coat School, London

My Tongue

I separate my life into different worlds.
One where I am British
Another where I am Bengali
Maintaining my traditions and cultures;
Making sure never to mix the two
At school, with my friends
I speak English, because it is easier
There is less hassle.

Talking with anyone outside my home parameters
I am forced to use it,
When I see it as a pointless means of communication;
When I would rather be left to my thoughts.
I walk among my fellow classmates
Only to be considered, I'm far from one.

I feel the grasp of this language weakening by the hour . . .
Because I speak the slang equivalent of Bengali.
I feel inadequate, not worthy
The shell of the boy I once used to be.
My world's upside down
I will soon be left with one
And lose the other.

Bengali is in my blood
Stronger and greater.

Fiery and passionate
Fighting against the suppression
My mother tongue will stand firm
Never lost, never strained
Realising its divine beauty
Transforming my insecurities and vulnerabilities in life
Into ecstatic beauty, bringing joy
One deep and lasting pleasure.
Finally finding happiness as I accept my true destiny
It will always be deep within me, for eternity.
It has to be.

Fahim Rahman (15)
Sir John Cass Foundation & Red Coat School, London

Cocoon

In my cocoon I sit and bake
While conscious thoughts pass through my head
Still and quiet, I am awake

In my cocoon I sit and make
Dreams that form like rising bread
Outside sits life I cannot take

Still and quiet, I lie awake
I ponder things that they have said
And feel inside me that deep ache

In my cocoon I cry and quake
I long for anger, cold and red
To tear me free, cocoon will break

Quiet and still outside the lake
Pulls me closer on a thread
Someone hear me, I am awake!

In my cocoon, I dream, I bake
Those sinister thoughts to which I'm wed
My courage comes, it leaves, I flake
Still and quiet, I lie awake.

Meredith Bertasi (16)
The American School In London, London

We Are Meant To Be

(From a person who knows their own point of view)

I love it when you gaze into my eyes,
And the way you speak to me,
As we're daydreaming above, into the skies.

If there was a pod then we would fit in as one pea,
Because we work so well together.

When you hold my hand it's like the warmth from a mug of tea,
Even when you aren't there I can still feel the essence of you,
I'm so glad you're here with me.

If there was a pod then we would fit in as one pea,
Because we work so well together.

Every time I see your face,
I have a warm feeling inside,
My heart goes thump, thump at a certain pace.

If there was a pod then we would fit in as one pea,
Because we work so well together.

We work as one,
We never stay apart,
This is not like it's a con.

That is how I know we are meant to be.

Katherine Tweed (13)
The Clere School, Newbury

The Miners Stuck Below

Down in the humid and hot
Down there they have a whole lot
And yet they stay optimistic
Down in the dark and damp
They have nothing, not even a lamp
And yet they stay resilient
Little to do, little to eat
And surrounded by too much heat
And yet they stay charismatic
Scared of souls and the dark
With nowhere the space of a park
And yet they carry on hoping
Down there it's very claustrophobic
They could even be achluophobic
And yet they just carry on
And now they're coming out
With happiness they will shout
And then it will be over.

Eli Hatter (12)
The Clere School, Newbury

Football

Football, is a brilliant sport, some may say the best.
It is gargantuan where I live; is the one sport I would suggest.

I play for the local football team, it is pretty good,
The melancholy expression on the team's faces
Covered in thick, black mud.

I watch the mind-blowing jaw-gaping sport over and over again,
I watch it on TV and play it on the XBox,
I also write down all the scores with my hard-working pen.

I would like to play with the greats, like Messi, Ronaldo and Zidane,
They are truly fantastic, amazing, I am the biggest football fan.

The World Cup, the World cup,
The competition I would love to grace,
But for now it's back to the Sunday League,
Scoring a gob-smacking brace.

Nicholas Tate (12)
The Clere School, Newbury

Don't Change Me

I am who I am, you can't change me,
Within myself, you will see

I can't change who I am,
A lively, exuberant person was always the plan

I am irrepressible, don't change that,
No one can put me down, that's a fact!

Victoria Chappell (12)
The Clere School, Newbury

The Night

Under the moonlight my body lies,
Gazing up at the cloudless skies.
At my feet the campfire roars,
In the tent my brother snores.
In the trees the birds are sleeping,
On the hills the wolves are creeping.
Hoot go the owls, up in the night sky,
Witches on broomsticks are whizzing by.

Chloe Long (12)
The Clere School, Newbury

What Matters To Me

One of the things that matters me is sport
And some that I like to play are on a court,
Like tennis and squash, both played with a ball
And cricket and swimming and lots of football.

Another thing that matters to me is family,
Like parents and sisters and my Aunt Natalie,
When they're loving and caring and help me
But not when they made me get stung by a bee.

And the final thing that matters to me
Is a dream to gets lots of money,
A dream to have fun and do really well
And lots of wishes I may not want to tell.

Luke Skeels (12)
The Clere School, Newbury

Entertaining

What matters to me is entertaining,
I find it a lot of fun.
It covers a lot of areas,
Fine wine or cooking a bun.

But one thing I really like,
Is of course magic.
Pick a card, any card,
Magicians are charismatic.

I also like to cook up a plate
Of Italian fine cuisine.
I try not to make it fattening,
To keep my guests tall and lean.

To be a good host you have to be
Polite, kind and clean.
Lay the table, clean up the mess,
Hold the door when they leave.

You could even play some music,
Classical or rock.
But here is one handy tip,
I would recommend an iPod dock

Matthew Pawley (12)
The Clere School, Newbury

Emotions

Happiness, pleasure, contentment and joy,
Are many things that I enjoy.
Sadness, misery, depression and woe,
Make me feel at an all time low.
Surprise, amazement, astonishment and shock,
Make me OK if I take a knock.

Horror, fear, anxiety and fright,
Are many things that don't come with delight.
Anger, frustration, fury and hate,
Are some of the things that make you lose mates.
Nervousness, tension, apprehension and dread,
Put ghastly thoughts in my head.

Emotions, emotions, as you can see,
Are what make up you and me!

Louise Collins (12)
The Clere School, Newbury

A Lonely Soul

With hands dirty and cracked,
With eyelids heavy and red,
A man sat in old rags.

Begging for money, as people pass,
Some people were generous, some didn't care,
Time's never easy, time's always hard,
In times of hunger and thirst he always has to ask.

People may find it humorous,
That's sad in my eyes,
What he needs most is warmth, love, support and care,
Don't just stop and stare!

Jemma Mead (12)
The Clere School, Newbury

Dreams And Imagination

I frequently occur, time and time again.
There rarely goes a day without me being used.
I act like your mind's eye, your heart's desire,
A soul without me has no thoughts, no emotion too.

The vision I bring can be experienced by all,
Trances, pure and evil!
Your mind decides the secrets, they then steer the way,
Glance, peek, seek and glimpse
Will last a lifetime and thrive in moments similar to this.

The tears I shed feel that pain,
Never to be told.
I capture you each and every way,
I am natural, in your instinct,
I am dream and imagination!

Elizabeth Wilcox (12)
The Clere School, Newbury

Rugby

Rugby is my passion, rugby is my life,
I live to feel the ecstasy, I live to fight the fight.
Every Wednesday evening, every Sunday morning,
Come rain or shine, sleet or snow,
I've battled through it all.
If I were incapable or running,
If I were scared of the scrums,
I wouldn't know what to do with myself,
I'd simply be alone.
Whenever I am happy, whenever I am sad,
There's one thing I will always love
And that one love, my one love is rugby!

Barnaby Smeddle (12)
The Clere School, Newbury

The Seasons Matter

The majestic trees,
Rocking side to side,
The river flowing,
So gently, without a tide.

But it changes,
The soft snow falls,
White glaciers surround me,
Soaring snowballs.

But once again
The mood differs,
Orange leaves swirl around,
But it still makes you shiver.

Now it's different,
New creatures come alive,
The trees grow flower buds,
The bees rebuild their hives.

So what matters to me
Do you ask?
It's a really simple answer,
It's the world,
Changing colour,
The seasons
While they last.

Natasha Everest (12)
The Clere School, Newbury

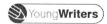

The Bike

The door of the shed opens,
Light shines in,
Excitement courses through me,
My wheels begin to spin.

I'm out in the open at last!
Where will we go today?
Over the hills to the common?
Or down to the park to play?

My owner comes and climbs aboard,
Her feet begin to pedal,
I want to join the cycle club,
Because sometimes you win a medal.

We cycle down the road
And begin to climb the hill,
We pass the woods and churchyard,
It gives me such a thrill.

Soon we must go home though,
Evening's on its way,
Back down past the hill, past the church,
Until another day.

Jessica Emberlin (13)
The Clere School, Newbury

Tennis

As I go in for the serve,
I smack the ball with some nerve.

I wear a T-shirt not a jacket
And fling the ball with a racquet.

I wish to play like Andy Murray
And if I win, celebrate with delicious rice and curry.

As I whack the ball with some spin,
I hope this power shot will make me win.

Over the net and on the floor,
I've won the game, there is no need to play anymore.

Since I won the spectacular, magnificent game,
I might gain some gigantic jaw-opening fame.

The exhilaration keeps me going,
My name will soon be worth knowing.

Edwin Edwards (12)
The Clere School, Newbury

Friends

Friends are forever there for you,
And are always affectionate
and kind hearted

They laugh, joke, share secrets with you and never let you down.

They tell you the truth and stay honest with you
throughout your friendship

But if you discover your friend has let you down
Has spread secrets and rumours that could hurt you
Humiliated and embarrassed you

You then sit and wonder whether they truly are your friend
A friend is always there for you, right until the end.

Ffion Donoghue (12)
The Clere School, Newbury

The Impossible

Deafening silence, louder than resounding thunder,
Sunlight drenching a screaming planet in waves of steel,
Ecstatic sorrow pulsing over a lifeless meadow,
Impossible.

Calm terror in the face of hideous beauty,
Cowardly courage agreeing to disagree,
Abundant poverty for the richly poor,
Impossible.

Stationary orbit around a cold sun,
An unacceptable solution to an understood mystery,
Artificial nature, fiery ice, icy fire,
Impossible.

Angelic demons and demonic angels,
Painless agony and confused logic,
Standing within harmonious discord,
Impossible.

Believe in the impossible,
Believe and you will know.
Don't let anyone tell you
Impossible!

Katherine Best (12)
The Clere School, Newbury

My List

I have a list of things that
Are important to me
But in this poem I shall
Mention my top three

First on the list has to be food
If I don't get enough
I get in a mood

Mum is the second
She's a really good chef
And she shouts dinner!
It's the only time I'm not deaf!

Last, but not least
Are my two pugs
They are like me
If they don't get their dinner
They turn into thugs.

Toby Carter (12)
The Clere School, Newbury

The Journey And What's To Come

Those cold, grubby hands clasp me,
He puts me under the screen,
The big bright light shines in my eyes,
I know he's looking at my person's face,
But it feels like they're interrogating me.

Finally, I'm pushed back into the warm, clean hands of my owner!

After that long, cold journey,
I'm put back in the travel section of the drawer,
Right where I belong.

With my friends,
With my family,
With the boarding passes I know and adore,
Madrid, San Francisco, Paris, Rome.

This is where I feel safe,
But most importantly at home.

In the middle of my life,
Fear of what's to come,
Where will I go and what will they do?
All these questions ringing in my cover.

But as my mum said, 'It's the present that matters.'
So onto that thought my cover pops.

The question to which I need an answer,
Where will I go next?

Shhh . . .

'So how do you fancy going to Fuertaventura next summer?'
'Oh yes, that sounds great!'

My question answered!

Now what should I pack . . . ?

Alexandra Humphreys [12]
The Clere School, Newbury

Dreams, Future And Imagination

Dreams matter to me.
When I may look absent minded,
My mind is really buzzing with thought,
Filling me with inspiration, bursting my imagination.

Future matters to me,
Although it may seem far away,
My choices change every day,
I hope for a perfect future, but who knows what it holds.

Imagination matters to me,
It may be only a small gaze,
Yet manage to lead me into a world of adventure,
Imagination allows me to explore,
What would I do without it?

Chloe Bryan (12)
The Clere School, Newbury

What Matters To Me - The Countryside

As I step into the fresh air
I walk along so it whispers through my hair.
I climb up the hills into the emptiness of the field,
Birds fly around my head as the dog races for pheasants.
The trees talk to me as the music in my head escapes.
I run across the landscape, as I feel the fresh breeze.
I never want to leave this paradise.
I don't usually think about what is waiting for me at home.
I have some company, just me and my dog,
A soulmate by my side.
Just paradise.

Maddie Christy (11)
The Clere School, Newbury

Dreams

There is a place that matters to me.
I travel there when I am sleeping.
In this place there are enchanted woods,
Beautiful flowers dancing in the crisp, cold breeze,
Crystal spider's webs glistening in the hazy sun,
Shimmering streams lay across the never-ending valleys,
Patchwork fields smother the land where I am.

But sometimes the land in which I stay, can turn.
A malevolent curse is struck upon my wonderful land,
Innocent trees are suffocated by this evil doom,
Spring buds burst with coldness,
This horrible truth is from the vulgar weather.

As the gloom fades into the distance, my precious land returns.
Bees buzz in perfect melody to the tune of the whistling wind,
The sweet morning chorus of song birds greets me,
So my peaceful kingdom, which I own,
Is back as I slowly awake.

Mollie Lawrence (12)
The Clere School, Newbury

The Shores Of Life

I lay entrapped by fear,
As icy shards caressed the shiver that lay dormant on my back,
White horses were galloping along the stretch of beach,
As if to lick the very essence of my sun-kissed feet.

My heart beat like a brass band, my lungs reached for respiration,
My brain was vivid with the sheer velocity of the unreal sight
That was perched before me.

My heart eclipsed as love was noticed
As a memory that no longer existed,
Birds of time flew high above the clouds in a sweet melody
Of the past that wished to be forgotten.

Faces were deathly and they wandered through time
To haunt the living,
The darkness shrouded me in a veil of gloom,
Upset roared inside me as I waited for revenge.
My boat of feeling sailed softly on the sea of love
And the tranquillity jaded all discontent.

Grace Goslin (12)
The Clere School, Newbury

The Wolf

As fast as a cheetah, it darted through the forest,
The dark, mysterious forest.
Its powerful body leaping over fallen logs,
The deer was blissfully unaware of the fast coming danger
And blissfully walked on.

The graceful creature let out a howl,
A bloodcurdling sound and ran on,
The deer was still, unaware of the unseen predator
Heading towards it at the fastest speed.

Once again, the creature leapt high into the air,
Not pausing to catch its breath,
The wolf bit down on its latest victim.

Megan Broughton (13)
The Clere School, Newbury

Animal's Imagination

Cheeky cats.
Caring crocodiles,
Overjoyed octopus,
Terrified tigers
Lovely lions,
Perfect pigs,
Magical mice,
Enchanting elephants.
Gorgeous giraffes,
Crazy camels,
Petrified penguins,
Outrageous owls,
Awful ants,
Hilarious hippos,
Beautiful bears,
Weird whales,
I love animals and hopefully they like me!

Anna Maria Markiewicz (12)
The Clere School, Newbury

What Matters To Me

What matters to me?
What, what matters to me?
Music is what matters to me
Rap, pop, both types of music
Now let's listen to the beat so you can move your feet!
Woo! Yeah, yeah!

What matters to me?
What, what matters to me?
Friends are what matters to me
Louis, James, both my friends
Make sure our homework's done, so we can have some fun!
Come on now.

Move your feet
Listen to the beat
Hang with your friends
And make sure you're wearing the trends!

Theo Canes (11)
The Clere School, Newbury

Afghanistan

All of the soldiers in Afghanistan
Fighting for their people,
Getting injured and hurt,
Hoping and praying for the day it all ends.
All of their families waiting in fear,
Night by night, endless bad dreams,
If their friends or relatives don't come back.
Some will never be happy again,
Terror and anguish.
Although they try to be brave,
Never quite knowing if they are safe and sound.

Catherine Wellington (11)
The Clere School, Newbury

Proud To Be British

Britain, Britain, such a wonderful place,
With butlers and tea and oh, so much grace.
Here created King Arthur and Robin Hood too
And once more, with some genius - Winnie The Pooh!

The journey for Britain begins 1066,
The Battle of Hastings, was it all just a fix?
The French beating the British, it's simply absurd,
Or maybe the story relayed, but misheard?

The next point on my list, 1583,
When Queen Elizabeth sent the sailor, Humphrey,
He sailed and sailed until he arrived,
To find nothing but rock; the land was deprived.

After losing America, East Africa too,
Britain still owned Canada and Nauru.
Britain was now booming, one third of the world,
But all of a sudden a dark thing unfurled.

Yes, World War I or the Great War to some,
My, what had Germany suddenly become?
But as usual, we won, as we expected to,
Then we all went home and made up a brew.

No sooner had one stopped had another began,
Once more with the Germans, but we had a plan.
We let them get all the way up to France
And from thereon we beat them and did a small dance!

Then, with the world not at war, Britain once again grew,
But sadly for Britain the wind no longer blew.
The Empire was over with Hong Kong it was,
But that was our Britain's final applause.

Since then nothing's happened, nothing at all,
Except Tony Blair, (yes, that utter fool).
Britain stepped aside and the world turned obscene,
The madness of a world now controlled by machine.

Thomas Hall (13)
The Clere School, Newbury

Arboretum

What wonders beauty can behold,
From malevolent eyes prying for secrets,
Stunning splendour, magnificently carved,
Majestic glory, caught within a golden pebble.

Within a single spark of fire,
Lies the future, past and present.

Tendril fingers grasping up,
Towards the midnight, numb with cold,
Spiralling, spinning, loving the dance,
Glittering life and fanatical fronds.

Within a single spark of fire,
Lies the future, past and present.

Exquisite beauty sprawled before me,
Blunt and dry, pinpricked with diamonds,
Embraced in a sea of sapphires,
Bedding in glittering emeralds.

Within a single spark of fire,
Lies the future, past and present.

Silhouetted on flawless perfection,
Dazzling bright in a whistle of breeze,
Reflected twice on a vanished mirror,
A fairy picture Nature had drawn.

Within a single spark of fire,
Lies the future, past and present.

Mystic shadows, dappled light,
Dormant slumber roams this world,
Alive with death, fringed with glass,
Crisp and vivid, cold wind bites.

Within a single spark of fire,
Lies the future, past and present.

Gnarled fingers snatch for freedom,
Sinister engravings, scratched and worn,
Smudged with fear and arctic thoughts,
Ghostly veils draped over a hostile landscape.

Within a single spark of fire,
Lies the future, past and present.

Death was close, end was nigh,
Nightmares tore through every hour,
Time just dragged, frozen and suspended,
The axe was swung, the whole world trembled.

Within a single spark of fire,
Lies the future, past and present.

Ashes lay beyond this place,
Elusive, vague and clearly forgotten,
Still lives the love, a memory past,
Coldest of fires, still enchantingly intense.

Within a single spark of fire,
Lies the future, past and present.

Sarah Ladd (12)
The Clere School, Newbury

Time

Time is a precious thing, you can only have it once.

Hands may hold it, minds can save it
And remember it, and hatred destroys it.

There is no life without time,
There is no end without time.

Time is the means and more than cause and effect.
Time can be changed, minor or major,
Time will end all things, but only at the end.

What you do with time is yours to decide;
You can make the most fantastic times,
The most confusing times,
The most dangerous times
And the best of times.

The thing about time,
Enjoy it while it lasts.
Don't let it pass you by too fast,
Keep clinging onto that mast
And someday you will find the past.

Reached and restored, the burning past;
Keep holding onto that mast.
Maybe time just flows too fast,
Don't let go of the good old past.

Rosie King (13)
The Clere School, Newbury

Inspirational, Individual Dreams

A river of imagination,
Bursting at the seams,
A fountain of changing desire,
Desperate to be seen.

A persuasion like hint,
Guiding your options,
And undiscovered path to take,
To change a life forever . . .

To be seen, but with blinded eyes,
Understood in interpretation,
A choice, a change,
An inspiration.

Elke Abinger (12)
The Clere School, Newbury

What Matters To Me

What happened to tree houses?
The climbing, the building, the fun.
Now we're told to be careful,
Take a coat,
Don't touch that!

We might have a computer game,
Which are never quite the same,
The buttons, the images, the clicks,
Plenty of experience,
But where's the hands on fun?

What happened to the happy children?
The place they called their own?
Oh! I remember now, an invasion of hard hats,
Heavy, protective goggles and a fluorescent jacket
Swallowed up our fun.

Alexandra Winter (13)
The Clere School, Newbury

Best Friends Matter To Me

I'll always be at your side,
Until the very end,
Wiping all your tears away,
Being your best friend.
I'll smile when you smile,
I'll feel the same pain
And if you cry a single tear
I promise I will too.

I will always be your partner in crime,
Whenever you are lost,
I will sit with you until the end of time,
Even if it's in the frost.
I won't judge you on what I hear,
You wouldn't do that to me,
Whatever you do,
I will always love you, no matter what.

You have been at my side
Through good and bad,
So words could never express
How I'd feel if I made you feel sad.
I'm here to lift you up when you're down,
Making you laugh instead of wearing a frown.
Our friendship is genuine and true,
I know this because I'll be beside you.

I'll never leave you
Stranded, on your own,
I can't imagine life without you,
I'll be here when you need a hug,
When you're on the floor with your heart bleeding,
I'll be there you pick up your pieces.

Zoe Baronius Bevan [13]
The Clere School, Newbury

258

Grandad

My brother never knew you,
My father mourned you,
Soul-shatterer.
You were gone too soon,
You saw the first landing on the moon,
Star-gazer.
You said you'd help. Too late,
You found your soulmate,
Heart-breaker.
Gran doted on you,
Gran told you to stop too,
Mind-maker-upper.
And now I still cry,
I want to be with you and die,
Grandad.

Katie Scott (15)
The Clere School, Newbury

Extinction Of Polar Bears

In a forgotten paradise a polar pup just sits and cries,
While far away, in another land its mother is hunting for a seal pup.
But the ice breaks beneath her feet,
Another life has ended.

In a forgotten paradise a polar pup just sits and cries,
Why do we do this? Why don't we care?
This matters to me
And I hope it matters to you.

Justine Whitehead (11)
The Clere School, Newbury

Cake

Cake, cake, lovely cake,
Loads of different types of cake,
Carrot cake, chocolate, strawberry, sponge,
Loads for you.

Cake, cake, loads of cake,
Big cakes, little cakes,
Wedding or birthday,
There's always one for you.

Cake, cake, different cakes,
You can bake for yourself!
Shelf to shelf, piled higher,
Higher than the sky!

Cake, cake,
I love them all,
Especially with the icing piled high.

Luke Williams (11)
The Clere School, Newbury

Happiness For Me

A laugh, a smile, a giggle, a poke,
A tickle, a chuckle, a smirk, a joke.
Something that gets me through the day,
I wouldn't have it any other way.

A friend, a foe, a mum, a dad,
A pet, a mate, a thing, a lad,
Someone or something that makes me smile,
Always means it's worthwhile.

I couldn't go without a laugh,
Even if I spilt my sides in half.
A thing that matters to me,
Why don't you guess, what could it be?

Katie Sainsbury (14)
The Clere School, Newbury

The Life Of Liverpool FC

Can't we go back to the days
Where the bricks just got laid?
When Shankly was in charge
And the dreams were very large?

Benitez was soon the man
Of this high dreaming Liverpool clan.
When the dreams were shortly over
Caused by the blue and white Blackburn Rovers.

Hodgson was now the boss
He is nothing but a doss.
Now 18th in the Premiership
Surely no one will envy this?

Now we are in the real day
And I just want to say,
Buy us you Boston Red Sox
Or continue on the heavy going mocks.

Tom Price (14)
The Clere School, Newbury

What Matters To Me

Piercing, green eyes staring at me,
Wondering if fish is on the menu for tea,
Confidently stepping out into the light,
Smiling cheekily in delight.
Silver whiskers and black paws
And a crazy tail, swishing between two doors,
Purring lovingly whilst sitting on the mat,
I really do love you, my little black cat.

Faye Lillywhite-Buley (11)
The Clere School, Newbury

What Matters To Me

What matters to me? I do not know.
There is nothing I can see that makes my heart glow.
What matters to me? Who can say?
There is nothing in this world for which I would pay.

What matters to me? What can I do?
I cannot find anything after which I would go.
What matters to me? Who can tell?
I cannot find anything I would not sell.

What matters to me? There is not even one
Thing I would hide from the sight of a gun.
What matters to me? What can I write?
What would I run after all through the night?

What matters to me? How long must I think?
And yet there is something that steals me a wink.
What matters to me? How about this thing I've espied?
Could it be found before all thought of it dies?

What matters to me? This thing I have found,
I *will* track it down, from the sky to the ground.
What matters to me? That which I do not despise.
The friendship of others is all I do prize.

Christopher Spence (13)
The Clere School, Newbury

In The News

Wake up in the morning,
Alarm at 7.
News on the telly,
Been bombing in Devon.

Suicide in Paris,
Terrorists in Iraq,
Why can't the world
Get together its act?

Why don't we hear
About birthdays and cake,
What about holidays
Instead of drowning in lakes?

I want to enjoy
What life gives to me,
I don't want to know
About money and greed.

Megan Dalgarno (13)
The Clere School, Newbury

What Matters To You

Don't you just hate it when you sit at the PC
And the computer freezes?
Do you know what I mean?

It sometimes says,
'System Error', but no more.

I think, I need a new PC,
But thinking of my luck
It's just playing with me.

It's annoying when it says,
'Cannot connect to the Internet'.
I wait a few minutes (that's a lot of time),
Then it says,
'Cannot connect online'.

Why did they invent a computer?
It's all a waste of time!

James Medcraft [11]
The Clere School, Newbury

Chocolate Cake

The perfect treat,
It tastes ever so sweet,
And also a joy to bake.
Soon you will see,
What else it could be,
Besides a chocolate cake.

The best thing to eat;
It cannot be beat,
Coated in chocolate shavings,
For such a small fee,
It nourishes me
And fulfils all my cravings.

The chocolatey filling,
(So long as you're willing),
Makes it worth the while.
You'll eat it with haste
And savour its taste
And it's certain to bring out a smile.

Coated with icing,
What could be more enticing,
When the texture's just right?
You'll have to persist;
Since who could resist
A chocolate cake delight?

It makes an invasion,
To every occasion,
Because it tastes so nice.
It's better than pie - don't ask me why,
So why not grab a slice?

John Anderson (13)
The Clere School, Newbury

Music, How It Makes You Feel

Music makes me happy
It makes me pump my fists
Music calms me down
It makes me ecstatic

Electronic dance has me going
Jazz makes me hurl
Hip-Hop makes me wanna dance
And love gets me flowing

I love singing
It is fantastic
I love music
It makes you feel great!

Jack Allen (11)
The Clere School, Newbury

Detention

Th sun shines on
My face, as I look
Through the window,
I feel the pain,
Detention again.

'You're a disgrace,'
He said to my face.
'I'm sorry Sir
That I sent him flying,
It's all my fault that he's now crying.'
'Go now Lad,
Say you're sorry,
As you did push him
Into that quarry!'

Aisha Baizid (11)
The Clere School, Newbury

What Matters To Me

What matters to me is my family, they support me and stick up for me, just like my friends.
I like to listen to music, all you can hear through my walls is music, which shakes just like an earthquake.

What matters to me is my future, I don't want to mess up like my brother, I don't want to lie and I want time to fly during school.

What matters to me is sport . . .
Football rules, Chelsea are the best, I am shouting for them to win.
Rugby, painful but I still get stuck in.
Tennis, well let's say Andy Murray's the best, quick ball, 155mph, I hope to be as good as him one day or another.
I love to run and watch TV and my favourite moment was watching Usain Bolt, the fastest thing running, beat the world record.
Formula 1 is however the best sport ever. Lewis Hamilton and Jensen Button make the greatest team yet.

That's what matters to me . . .

Louis Hooper (11)
The Clere School, Newbury

Epiphany

All I am is a fleeting existence.
I peer out, somewhat hesitantly
As I proceed forward.

Forward, tentatively.
Forward, devotedly.
Forward I go.

Am I to understand my role?
A being placed here
Dutiful, yet naïve.

Dreams, desires, hope.
Fantasies of a
Lost imagination.

We desire knowledge
The pure realisation
Of our reason to be.

They speak of the divine.
A celestial entity.
Yet do they truly know?

They preach of our calling;
The twisted hand of
Fate looms upon us.

My knowledge is this

I am today.
I am not tomorrow.
Yesterday, I never was.

I am nothing
To a higher supremacy
Than I.

All I am is a
Fleeting existence.

Claudia Fuller (17)
The Isle of Wight College, Newport

At 9

When I was young,
Somebody told me,
That all the stars in the sky,
Were all the people in Heaven.

When I was young,
Somebody told me,
To pull their finger.

When I was young,
Somebody told me,
To be brave and wear a smile,
That it would all be over soon,
And only take a short while.

Now that you're a star,
I wonder if you saw,
How brave I tried to be,
While staring at the floor.

The men carried the box,
Then set it on a stand,
And all the tales were told,
Of a well-loved man.

When it was all over
As short as I was told,
All I wanted was a cuddle,
I've never felt so cold.

Now that I am older
I understand much more,
To never pull a finger
Or believe all I am told.

When I reach the end,
Upwards I will fly,
We'll shine all night together
Up in the clear, dark sky.

Lydia Freya Lawrence Lee (16)
The Isle of Wight College, Newport

A Sea Of Golden Dreams

An endless sea of gold,
A crisp, dry ocean,
An endless expanse you cannot begin to withhold,
That can draw up the furthest emotion,
Or the closest dream.

You reach out to touch,
And let out a smile,
This is something that you cannot clutch,
For it is beyond a mile,
Beyond one's limitless imagination.

Pictures cannot begin to explain,
The scene before your eyes,
Many painters have tried in vain,
To draw this beautiful prize,
But this is something that's for only the mind.

The shining sun begins to set,
The glow of the golden sea begins its retreat,
Dull, brown stalks leave you upset,
You are left without any heat
Apart from that in your memory . . .

Michael Sims (17)
The Isle of Wight College, Newport

Lost In Time

I spent a childhood held hostage by my emotions
Hovering under a black cloud
Wishing it would stop controlling me
Living in a straightjacket
Nowhere to run and hide
All around were brick walls

Every night was a day
Every day was a night
Time would speed past
I could no longer hold the strings
Slowly I lost parts of myself
Watching them disappear

Invisible strength appeared
The black cloud began to lighten
The brick wall grew weak
The pain no longer grew deep
A bright sun appeared and embraced me
I saw a way out, alive.

Rachael Wade (18)
The Isle of Wight College, Newport

Call You Mine

Not a fraction of a second that look did take,
Filled with passion, but drenched in hate.
But with my heart and with my mind,
Neither one of them remained aligned.

Two parallel lines.
No, but they cross.
And with each they both define,
These two humans - do not undermine.

A straight divide prevents the peace,
Causing disruption along the crease
And as those lines stay with their ties,
Hereby remains that hating despise.

Oh, but they can love.
Tell them. They want to.
But the secret is held in,
Within the wall of the most sacred.
It stays.

For years they lived in uncertainty.
Friends they were, until touched by reality.
Too much love had created hate,
And in the end, it was too late.

Time passes and they meet again,
Driven away but brought back.
The past is the past. Forgotten.
This a new leaf, a new pattern.

Realisation hits.
They never knew what they were,
Without the other.
They are consoled. One, whole.

Not a fraction of a second that look did take.
Filled with passion, but drenched, in hate.
For now those lines have become equal, aware.
Uncrossed, they understand, this love has been declared.

And for now, we say farewell.
New futures created, we'll see, excel.
From confusion and hate, to the misread signs,
It gives me relief to believe that
I can finally, call you mine.

Karen Elliott (16)
The Isle of Wight College, Newport

Just Me

Swinging. Enchanting, rhythmic, focused.
Motion lulled the long forgotten limbs.
Numbing. Numbing. Please, please.
Eyes insistent on glaring at the fidgeting.
I'm so sorry eyes, shoot daggers and judge;
I have no say in this.

What about my hands?
They are there too, although . . . I don't want them to be.
Forget. Forget. Please, please.
Eyes have found them, no hiding it seems.
I'm so sorry eyes, tell me I'm stupid;
I have no say in this.

I want to leave them be.
It's better than remembering them, feeling them.
Stop. Stop. Please, please.
Eyes can't see me here, in the confines of my skull.
Only room for one you know;
He doesn't.

Nevertheless
I'll swing
    I'll forget
        I'll carry on
I'll dig out the perfected photo album . . . and remember . . .
A time when my legs were mine, my hands were mine,
My body. Was mine.

Sarah Redrup (16)
The Isle of Wight College, Newport

Friendship

I'd rather be a pack of wolves,
Than be a big, cruel shark.
A pack of wolves will stick together,
But a shark will swim alone.

I'd rather be an orchestra,
Than be a soloist.
An orchestra will play together,
But a soloist plays alone.

I'd rather be a city,
That a small, forgotten village.
A city is crowds and noise and people,
But a village is quiet and lonely.

I'd rather be a friendship gang,
Than be me, myself, alone.
A friendship gang is what I have and will have for evermore,
The gang are the ones that give me the courage to be myself,
on my own.

I am both forever, forever, till I die,
If I were one it wouldn't be me.
If I were a friendship gang then I could never last on my own,
But if I were just me on my own, I'd be so very lonely.

Charlotte West (11)
The Wey Valley School, Weymouth

I'd Rather Be . . .

I'd rather be an elephant,
Than a mouse,
I'd rather be a boy,
Than a girl.

I'd rather be a sparrow,
Than a snail,
I'd rather be a hammer,
Than a nail.

I'd rather be happy,
Than be sad,
I'd rather be normal,
Than be mad.

But I am who I am,
And that's just life.

Paige Sewell (13)
The Wey Valley School, Weymouth

The World Is Our World

The world is our world,
The world is magic,
The world is creative,
We love our world,
We don't want to destroy it.

The wonders of it are unbelievable,
They are magical,
The world is our world,
It must be here forever,
Our world is dying.

And we're going with it.

Kay Conway-Smith (13)
The Wey Valley School, Weymouth

276

What Matters To Me (Tea)

What matters to me?
Who really knows?
Not me, not you,
Well, not fully, no.

I had trouble thinking
What I care about,
But then I realised,
Without a doubt.

I know what I am,
I know what I be
And what I like, well . . .
I love drinking tea!

The entire British Empire
Was built on cups of tea,
You can't go to war without one,
It's our nation's drink you see.

I'd drink it with a cake,
Or even a chocolate bar,
Anything goes well with
A nice, hot, cup of char.

I'll drink it with my mum and dad,
I love it with my nan,
I'll have it with my mates sometimes,
I just like it so much, man.

Well, tea you know, it's the best ever drink,
It's perfect for a cold winter night
And when you're feeling a little bit down
It makes you feel alright.

It's good for conversation,
'Come sit with my and my pot of tea.'
But best of all, as you can see,
It's just perfect for poetry.

Eliot Glanvill (16)
Torquay Boys' Grammar School, Torquay

#4

To repeat oneself is a sign of senility,
That is what my father once said,
Or twice, or thrice,
Or four or five times.
Come to think of it, he always repeated it.
'To repeat oneself is a sign of senility',
That's what my father told me, yes,
My mother gabbled an awful lot about
The state of the country and the education system;
And thus, remarkably, she liked to repeat herself;
(But not really in the same way).
I do try not to repeat myself,
But it is important to me to get my point across, because
I might not get heard, even though my father did once tell me, believe it or not,
That 'To repeat oneself is a sign of senility.'
Who'd have credited that, eh?
When Ma and Pa were gone, I found myself struggling;
Repetition became not so forthcoming; it swooned;
I swooned.
To repeat oneself is a sign of senility, by all accounts,
But I don't know, because,
If to repeat oneself were a sign of senility,
Would not a daily routine also become futile in the fight against repetition?
Nay, when you look at it,
To repeat oneself is a sign of security, of comfort,
Of a little boy lost in a world of rapid change.
IAmStillHereIAmStillHere IAm StillHere IAm StillHere I am
I am still   here I Am   still here I am
        stil

Joe Bennett (16)
Torquay Boys' Grammar School, Torquay

Young Writers Information

We hope you have enjoyed reading this book - and that you will continue to enjoy it in the coming years.

If you like reading and writing poetry drop us a line, or give us a call, and we'll send you a free information pack.

Alternatively if you would like to order further copies of this book or any of our other titles, then please give us a call or log onto our website at www.youngwriters.co.uk

Young Writers Information
Remus House
Coltsfoot Drive
Peterborough
PE2 9BF
(01733) 890066